Sorella's Kitchen

Compiled and Written by Rose Lambi

On the cover left to right:

Gussie, Rose, Baby Jeanette sitting on Norma DiMaggio's lap, Mary,
Virginia sitting on the chair, and Pearl. c. 1927

Sorella's Kitchen

Library of Congress Control Number 2005910593

ISBN 0-9724257-4-8
First Printing December 2005
Second Printing February 2006

Rose Lambi Publications
1515 Hibernation Hollow
Wentzville, MO 63385

Designed, printed, and bound in the United States of America by:
ImagineInk Publishing Company, Inc.
2178 East Pitman Avenue
Wentzville, MO 63385

A special thanks to the following family members who contributed recipes, photos, and love in making this recipe book a reality.

Rose Lambi
Mary Midiri
Betty Guccione
Norma Nichols
Jo Merklin
Gwen Guccione
Jim Guccione
Dawn Wilson

Thank you for purchasing our cookbook! With your purchase, you have helped the following organizations.

First Step Back Home - This organization helps the homeless men in Western St. Charles County to start a new productive life by accommodating meals, lodging and job assistance.

Green Lantern - This organization was started in 1971 in St. Charles County and continues to provide Meals on Wheels and activities for senior citizens in St. Charles County.

About DiMaggio

We are a group of cousins from the ancestors of the Salvatore DiMaggio family. Our grandpa, Salvatore DiMaggio, arrived in America in 1910 as a very young man. Our grandma, Norma Russo, arrived in America in 1912. They were married shortly after Grandma came through Ellis Island. They settled in St. Louis, Missouri, where our mothers were born and raised. There were six daughters born to Salvatore and Norma and from those six sisters, we learned some great recipes with the Sicilian flare.

The sisters were Maria (Mary), Rosa (Rose), Christina (Gussie), Providenz (Pearl), Antionette (Jeanette) and Vita (Virginia). Although all the DiMaggio sisters have left this world, our intentions are to share some of their great recipes and ours with you and have our memories of our childhood reborn.

Although some of these recipes came from our mothers, others were acquired as favorites from our friends and restaurants. We hope the following recipes will come as a welcomed addition to your cooking favorites.

DiMaggio Sisters: Jeanette, Virginia, Pearl, Gussie, Rose, and Mary. Baby Joe is on the ground.

Rose on the table while Mary looks at the cake.

Rose kissing Mary

Rose, Mary, Pearl, Virginia standing. Jeanette on Salvatore DiMaggio's lap.

Mary

Mary

Rose, Joe (Dad), and Mary

Rose and Mary

Rose

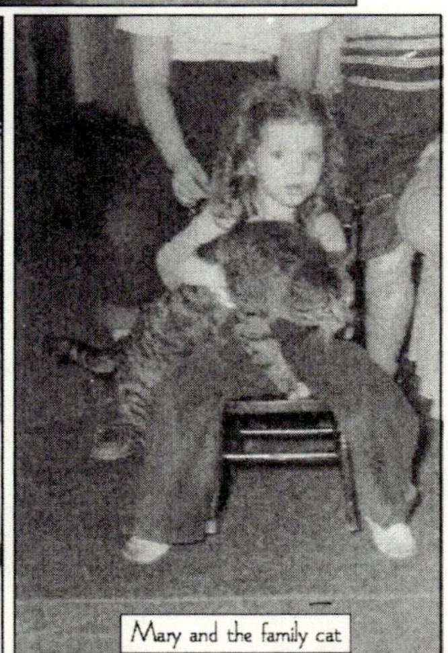

Mary and the family cat

BILLS OF FARE

APPETIZERS

▲ Place fresh or dried mint in the bottom of a cup of hot chocolate for a cool and refreshing taste.

▲ One lemon yields about 1/4 cup juice; one orange yields about 1/3 cup juice.

▲ Seeds and nuts, both shelled and unshelled, keep best and longest when stored in the freezer. Unshelled nuts crack more easily when frozen. Nuts and seeds can be used directly from the freezer.

▲ To prevent cheese from sticking to a grater, spray the grater with cooking spray before beginning.

▲ Fresh lemon juice will remove onion scent from hands.

▲ Instant potatoes are a good stew thickener.

▲ Three large stalks of celery, chopped and added to about two cups of beans (navy, borwn, pinto, etc.) will make them easier to digest.

▲ For tea flavoring, dissolve old-fashioned lemon drops or hard mint candy in your tea. They melt quickly and keep the tea brisk.

▲ Never soak vegetables after slicing; they will lose much of their nutritional value.

Apple Dip

Recipe from Mary Midiri

2 pkg. 8 oz. cream cheese
1 lb. brown sugar
2 tsp. vanilla
1 bag Heath Bits of Bricalle

Mix all together and slice apple to dip in.

Paula Dean's Artichoke Dip

Recipe from Dawn Wilson

2 cans artichoke hearts
1 pkg. frozen, chopped spinach
1/2 cup mayonnaise
1/2 cup sour cream
1 cup grated Parmesan cheese
1/4 cup pepper jack cheese

Drain artichoke hearts; add to food processor and pulse until chopped but yet chunky; add to large mixing bowl; heat spinach in microwave for 5 minutes; drain and cool. Add drained spinach to artichoke mixture; add mayo, sour cream, Parmesan cheese and stir well; add to baking dish; top with pepper jack cheese.

Bake at 350 degrees for 30 minutes until golden brown.

Bacon Cheese Dip

Recipe from Rose Lambi

8 oz. chive and onion cream cheese
8 oz. sour cream
1½ cups mayonnaise
1/3 cup bacon bits
16 oz. Swiss cheese, shredded

Mix well; fill cavity of Beer Bread (see recipe to right) and bake at 325 degrees for 20 to 30 minutes or until dip is golden and bubbly; let dip sit for 10 to 15 minutes before serving; place cubed bread around dish and dip bread or spoon onto bread cubes.

Note: Can make mixture and bread day before needed; simply fill cavity of bread when ready to bake with mixture and bake.

Serves a party. Your guests will want this recipe!

Beer Bread

2 cups self-rising flour
3 Tbl. sugar
1 can beer, at room temperature

Combine flour and sugar, add beer, stir with a wooden spoon; spoon into a loaf pan and let sit for 15 minutes (to make bread rise) before baking; bake at 350 degrees for 50 minutes; cool completely, then cut in 1" cubes to dip in Bacon Cheese Dip. If using bread cavity for baking and serving bowl, cut to 1" from edges, fill cavity with mixture and bake.

Note: To make self-rising flour: 2 cups all-purpose flour, 1 tsp. salt & 2 tsp. baking powder.

Italy is like cooked macaroni—yards and yard of soft tenderness, raveled round everything.

—D. H. Lawrence

Bacon Wrap Hot Appetizer

Recipe from Betty Guccione

1 loaf white bread with crust trimmed off
1 lb. bacon cut in half
Cream of Mushroom or Cream of Chicken soup,
undiluted

Lay the bread slices out on tray and spread soup on one side of bread; connect the opposite corners of the bread and wrap a half slice of bacon around and secure with a toothpick; bake in 350 degree oven until browned and bacon is fully cooked; serve hot.

Bailey's Irish Cream

Recipe from Mary Midiri

1 can Eagle Brand condensed milk
1 cup whipping cream
4 eggs
2 Tbl. chocolate syrup
2 tsp. instant coffee
1 tsp. vanilla extract
1/2 tsp. almond extract
1-3/4 cup Irish Whiskey

Blend until smooth; refrigerate; enjoy!

I drink to the general joy of the whole table.
—William Shakespeare, Macbeth

Basil & Tomato Feta Bruschetta

Recipe from Rose Lambi

1 loaf French bread, cut into ½" thick slices
2 Tbl. olive oil
1 lb. plum tomatoes, chopped (about 2½ cups)
4 oz. crumbled Feta Cheese with Basil & Tomato, finely
chopped
1/2 cup finely chopped red onion
3 Tbl. fresh parsley, chopped
1 Tbl. pitted ripe olives, chopped
1/4 tsp. pepper

Place bread on cookie sheet and broil until lightly toasted on both sides; brush 1 side of toasted bread lightly with 1 tablespoon oil. Meanwhile, mix tomatoes, remaining oil, cheese, onion, parsley, olives and pepper; spoon 2 teaspoons mixture onto each toasted slice just before serving.

Makes 36 servings.

Brie

Recipe from Dawn Wilson

2 lbs. brie
6 oz. frozen or fresh raspberries
1 cup sugar
½ cup Chamborou (raspberry liquor)

Trim the rind from brie; place the brie in a pie shell; place top of pie shell and squeeze edges together to form a seal; bake at 425 degrees for 20 minutes or until pie crust is golden brown.

Combine raspberries, sugar and Chamborou (raspberry liquor), in sauce pan and cook on low heat while stirring constantly until sugar is dissolved; pour over top of brie while warm. Serve with water crackers or French bread cubes.

Note: Can substitute Chamborou with Blackberry Liquor or Brandy or Amoretto.

Serves many.

Bruschetta

Recipe from Norma Nichols

**6 large thick slices of white bread, firm textured
or day old
3 cloves garlic
Salt and ground black pepper, to taste
1/2 cup extra-virgin olive oil**

Toast the bread in a preheated oven at 350 degrees until golden brown on both sides; rub each slice of toast with half a clove of garlic; sprinkle each slice with salt and pepper; drizzle each with oil and serve.

Serves 4 to 6.

No man is lonely while eating spaghetti—it requires so much attention.

—Anonymous

Mary's Cheese Ball

Recipe from Mary Midiri

**2 pkg. 8 oz. cream cheese
1 pkg. Budding corn beef, diced
1 bunch of green onions, diced
1 Tbl. garlic salt**

Mix all together and roll into a ball then roll into chopped pecans; refrigerate for 1 hour; serve with crackers.

Good and easy.

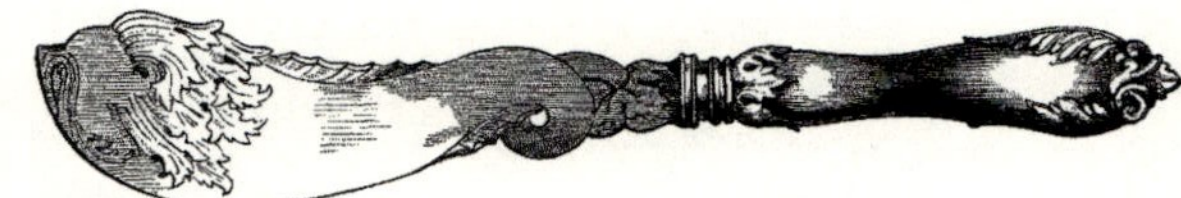

Caponata (Eggplant Appetizer)

Recipe from Rose Lambi

1 large eggplant
1 large white onion, chopped
2 ribs celery, stripped
5 Tbl. olive oil
15 green olives, chopped
3 Tbl. sugar

3 oz. capers
1 tsp. salt
2 cups Italian plum tomatoes, chopped
1/2 tsp. pepper
3 large cloves garlic, chopped
1/3 cup red wine vinegar

Cut eggplant, celery and onion into ¼" pieces; cut tomatoes into ½" pieces; in a large skillet, add olive oil, onions and garlic; cook on medium heat until the onions become translucent; add all remaining ingredients; simmer, stirring frequently until all the ingredients have thickened thoroughly; remove from heat and stir in the sugar; serve on lightly toasted Italian or French bread; Serve hot or cold.

Note: Will keep 2 weeks in refrigerator.

Makes about 5 cups.

Cracked Green Olive Salad

Recipe by Rose Lambi

3 lbs. Colossal green olives with pits
3 cups olive oil
7 cloves garlic, finely chopped
2 cups red wine vinegar
1-1/2 Tbl. dried oregano
1 Tbl. pepper
1-1/2 Tbl. dried basil
2 stalks celery, stripped & cut into 1/8" pieces

Crack olives on a cutting board with an unopened can or thick glass jar or bottle; place olives in a large bowl with all remaining ingredients and mix well; serve with Asiago or Fontinella cheese chunks and Italian bread to dip in the oil.

Note: Refrigerating overnight blends all the flavors nicely. This will last in the refrigerator for weeks.

Dill Dip

Recipe from Mary Midiri

1 round loaf pumpernickel bread
2/3 cup sour cream
2/3 cup mayonnaise
1 Tbl. parsley flakes
1 tsp. dill weed
1 tsp. dry minced onions
1 tsp. garlic salt
1 tsp. Accent seasoning
3 drops Tabasco sauce

Mix all ingredients except bread; when ready to serve make a cavity in the middle of bread; serve dip in cavity and use the extra pieces of bread to dip with.

Note: Best if dip sets for several hours or overnight.

Fresh Fruit Dip

Recipe from Jo Merklin

8 oz. jar marshmallow cream
8 oz. cream cheese
4 oz. sour cream

Combine ingredients in medium-size mixing bowl and blend until smooth.

Note: A drop of cherry juice makes a nice color for dipping strawberries.

Ham or Crab Pinwheel Appetizer

Recipe from Rose Lambi

1 pkg. super size flour tortilla
1/4 cup black olives, chopped
2 pkg. 8 oz. cream cheese, softened
2 pkg. 2-1/2 oz. each, sliced processed ham
1/2 cup mayonnaise
1/4 Tbl. green onions, chopped

Combine all ingredients except tortilla; spread mixture on tortilla; arrange 4 slices ham over cheese; tightly wrap in plastic wrap; refrigerate at least 3 hours or overnight; to serve, cut into ¾" slices.

Crab appetizer: Omit olives and ham. Add ¼ cup chopped red pepper; 1 cup shredded cheese; 5 oz. chopped imitation crab.

Mushroom Crostini

Recipe from Rose Lambi

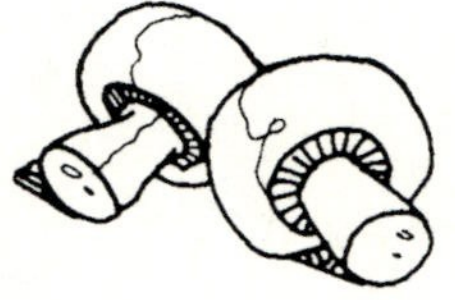

1 small or 1/2 large baguette
1 shallot, thinly sliced into rings
8 oz. Chanterellies or other wild mushrooms, coarsely chopped
12 rounds (1/4" thick) goat cheese, cut from a log (about 6 oz), room temperature
2 Tbl. extra-virgin olive oil, plus more for brushing
Coarse salt and freshly ground pepper

Preheat oven to 375 degrees; cut baguette crosswise into 12 quarter inch thick slices; place on a baking sheet; brush with oil; season with salt and pepper; toast in the middle of oven until golden, 8 to 10 minutes; remove and cool.

Heat 2 tablespoons oil in a medium skillet over medium heat; add shallot; cook, stirring until soft, about 3 minutes; add mushrooms, cook, stirring occasionally, until tender and any juices have evaporated (approximately 7 to 10 minutes); season with salt and pepper.

Place a round of goat cheese on top of each crostini; top with a tablespoon of mushroom mixture; sprinkle with chives.

Serve warm; serves 4 to 6.

Party Feta Appetizer

Recipe from Rose Lambi

1/2 cup mayonnaise
1/3 cup feta cheese
1 Tbl. green onions, finely chopped
1 Tbl. green pepper, finely chopped
1 Tbl. red pepper, finely chopped
12 party rye slices

Mix all ingredients except bread; toast 1 side of bread at 350 degrees; spread mixture on untoasted side; bake 1/1/2 to 2 minutes and serve hot.

Note: Can toast one side prior to a party; then when ready to serve, complete the recipe.

Makes 12 appetizers.

Party Pizza

Recipe from Mary Midiri

2 lbs. hot pork sausage
2 lbs. Velvetta cheese, cubed
1/2 cup catsup
2 tsp. oregano
1 tsp. powder garlic
2 loaves party rye bread

Brown sausage and pour off fat; add cheese, catsup, oregano and garlic; stir and cook for about 15 minutes; spread on 3 loaves of party rye bread; bake for 10 to 15 minutes in a 375 degrees oven.

Serves a party.

I feel a recipe is only a theme, which an intelligent cook can play each time with a variation.

—*Madame Benoit*

Veggie Pizza

Recipe from Mary Midiri

**1 pkg. crescent rolls
1/3 cup ranch dressing
8 oz. cream cheese, softened
1/2 pkg. hidden valley dry mix**

Spread crescent rolls on a 9 x 13 pan joining the perforated part together; bake according to directions; spread last 3 ingredients on cool crust; top with chopped broccoli, chopped cauliflower, shredded carrots, green onions, peppers, (red, green and yellow for color), black olives (sliced) or any desired vegi's you like; sprinkle finely shredded cheddar cheese; cut into squares. Good!

White Bean Dip

Recipe from Mary Midiri

**2 cans cannelli beans
3 Tbl. olive oil
Fresh mint
Garlic salt, to taste**

Blend together and enjoy on toasted bagette slices.

Note: Best if chilled for a few hours before serving.

Hot Artichoke Bake

Recipe from Rose Lambi

2 cans artichoke hearts, chopped
1 tsp. lemon juice
1 cup mayonnaise
1 pinch garlic powder or salt
1 cup Parmesan cheese
1/4 tsp. salt

Mix together and bake at 350 degrees for 25 to 30 minutes; serve with your favorite cracker or crostini bread.

Serves a party or large group.

A good cook is like a sorceress who dispenses happiness.
—*Elsa Schiaparelli*

BREADS and ROLLS

Weights and Measurements

Baking Powder
  1 cup = 5-1/2 oz.
Cheese, American
  1 Lb. = 2-2/3 Cup cubed
Cocoa
  1 Lb. = 4 Cups ground
Coffee
  1 Lb. = 5 Cups ground
Corn Meal
  1 Lb. = 3 Cups
Cracker Crumbs
  23 soda crackers = 1 Cup
  15 graham crackers = 1 Cup
Eggs
  1 egg = 1/4 Cup or 4 Tbl.
  4-5 whole eggs = 1 Cup
  7-9 whites = 1 Cup
  12-14 yolks = 1 Cup

Flour
  1 Lb. All-purpose = 4 Cups
  1 Lb. Cake = 4-1/2 Cups
  1 Lb. Graham = 3-1/2 Cups
Lemon Juice
  1 medium lemon = 2 to 3 Tbl.
  5-8 medium lemons = 1 Cup
Lemon Rind
  1 lemon = 1 Tbl. grated
Orange Juice
  1 medium orange = 2 to 3 Tbl.
Shortening or Butter
  1 Lb. = 2 Cups
Sugar
  1 Lb. Brown = 2-1/2 Cups
  1 Lb. Cube = 96 to 160 Cubes
  1 Lb. Granulated = 2 Cups
  1 Lb. Powdered = 3-1/2 Cups

Equivalents

3 tsp. = 1 Tbl.	10-2/3 Tbl. = 2/3 Cup	4 Cups = 1 quart	16 ounces = 1 pound
4 Tbl. = 1/4 Cup	12 Tbl. = 3/4 Cup	4 Quarts = 1 Gallon	32 ounces = 1 quart
5-1/2 Tbl. = 1/3 Cup	16 Tbl. = 1 Cup	8 Quarts = 1 Peck	8 oz. liquid = 1 cup
8 Tbl. = 1/2 Cup	2 Cups = 1 pint	4 Pecks = 1 Bushel	1 oz. liquid = 2 Tbs.

Beer Bread

Recipe from Rose Lambi

**2 cups self-rising flour
3 Tbl. sugar
1 can beer at room temperature**

Combine flour and sugar, add beer, stir with a wooden spoon; spoon into a loaf pan let sit for 15 minutes (to make bread rise) before baking; bake at 350 degrees for 50 minutes.

Note: To make self-rising flour: 2 cups all-purpose flour, 1 tsp. salt & 2 tsp. baking powder.

Certain dishes can quietly haunt your life.
—John Thorne

Bruscetta

Recipe from Mary Midiri

**French bagette, sliced 1/4 inch thick;
toasted with olive oil and garlic.**

**Top with:
6-8 diced tomatoes
1 Tbl. garlic
Fresh basil
2-3 Tbl. olive oil
1 tsp. balsamic vinegar**

Mix your toppings all together and spread on toast; enjoy!

Cheddar Artichoke Bake

Recipe from Rose Lambi

1 loaf French bread
3/4 cup shredded cheddar cheese
1/3 cup mayonnaise
1 tsp. lemon juice
2 jars marinated artichoke hearts, drained and chopped

Slice bread loaf lengthwise and bake 10 minutes at 450 degrees; let cool while preparing topping. Mix all ingredients other than bread and top on baked bread; bake 10 minutes or until topping is golden and bubbly. Cut each half into slices and garnish, if desired.

Garnish suggestions: Paprika, sliced red pepper or fresh herbs.

Serves 10 to 12

German Pancakes

Recipe from Mary Midiri

4 eggs
3/4 cup flour
1/4 cup sugar
3/4 cup milk
1/2 tsp. salt
1/4 tsp. cinnamon
1/4 cup butter
2 medium apples, sliced thin

Heat oven to 400 degrees; put round pan in oven to heat. Beat eggs, flour, milk and salt; remove pan from oven and put 2 tablespoons butter in pan to melt. Put apples on top of melted butter and pour batter over the apples; mix cinnamon and sugar together and sprinkle on top of batter and bake for 20 to 25 minutes. Dust with powdered sugar.

Homemade Dressing

Recipe from Rose Lambi

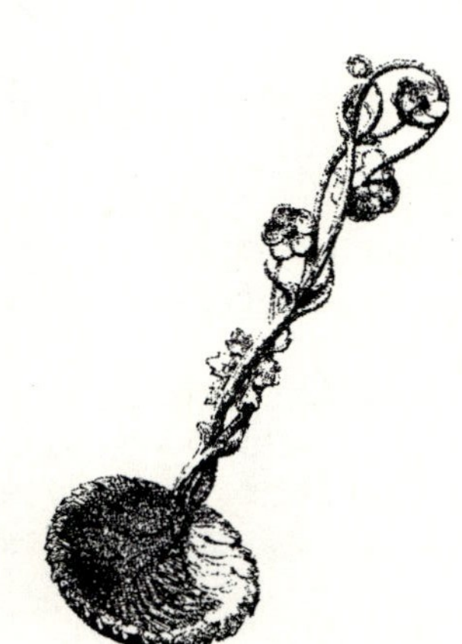

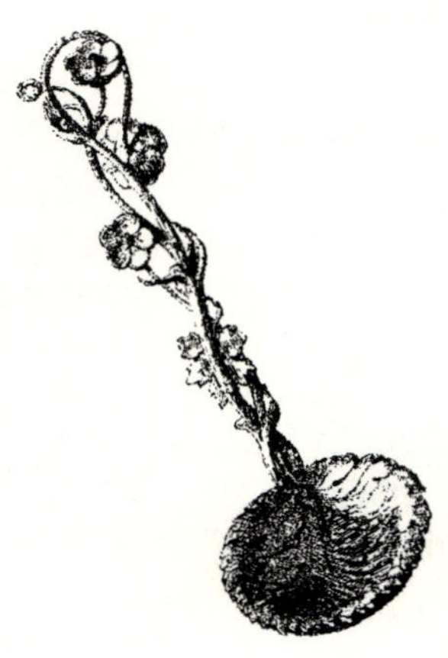

2 loaves of bread, cubed or 2 packages store stuffing mix
1 lb. sage pork sausage
4 Tbl. (1/2 stick) butter or margarine
3 to 4 stalks celery, stripped and diced
1 medium onion, chopped
2 cups chicken broth
Turkey gizzards, livers and heart
8 oz. mushrooms, thinly diced

Cube bread 1 to 2 weeks before needed; leave out on counter to dry out. In large skillet, fry sausage, stirring quite often to make the sausage very crumbly; drain off fat and add crumbled, cooked sausage to bread cubes. In pot, boil whole gizzards, livers and heart from turkey in 2 cups water; save broth for dressing; remove gizzards, livers and heart and finely chop when cool to the touch. In a large skillet melt butter and sauté celery, onions and mushrooms. Take a large mixing bowl (I use the turkey roaster) and place bread in bowl or pan; add sautéd celery, onions and mushrooms; add chopped gizzards, livers and heart; add broth, a little at a time until dressing is wet and moist; stuff turkey.

Note: If baking dressing in pan instead of cavity of turkey, make moister by adding more broth to dressing.

Yield: Enough dressing to stuff an 18 to 20 pound turkey

Italian Bread from Momma

Recipe from Rose Lambi

1 pkg. dry yeast
1/4 cup warm water
1-3/4 cup warm water
3 cup sifted flour
2 Tbl. salt
1-1/2 to 1-3/4 cup flour

Dissolve yeast in 1/4 cup warm water; let yeast stand 5 to 10 minutes. Meanwhile, put in large bowl 1-3/4 cup warm water and 2 tablespoons salt; blend in 3 cups flour; stir yeast and add to flour mixture mixing well. Measure 1-1/2 to 1-3/4 cups flour; add half the flour mixture to yeast mixture and knead until smooth. Mix in enough remaining flour to make a soft dough; place on a lightly floured surface; rest 5 to 10 minutes; knead.

Place in greased bowl; turn dough to bring greased side to top; let it sit for 1-1/2 to 2 hours. Then knead 2 minutes; divide in 2; let stand 10 minutes. Place in loaf pans; let stand until doubled. Bake at 425 degrees for 10 minutes; reduce temperature to 350 degrees; bake 1 hour taking bread out of pans and placing directly on oven rack the final 20 minutes.

Serve warm with butter or olive oil, pepper, salt and Parmesan cheese.

Makes 2 loaves.

Sausage Bread

Recipe from Rose Lambi

1 egg
1 lb. pork sausage
1 cup Parmesan cheese
1 loaf frozen bread dough, thawed
1 Tbl. butter, melted

Spray oil on bowl or pan while thawing bread to avoid sticking.

Brown pork sausage, drain. Mix sausage, cheese and egg in bowl; roll bread out flat (this will take some time as the bread will keep going back together). Spread mix on bread and roll into log shape. Place on cookie sheet with seam down; rub top with melted butter; bake at temperature indicated on bread instructions for about 25 to 30 minutes.

Note: May substitute Romano cheese instead of Parmesan, if you desire.

Sicilian Cheese Bread

Recipe from Rose Lambi

1 loaf Italian bread
Fresh ground pepper
Olive oil
1 can anchovies (optional)
1 cup grated Romano cheese

Preheat oven to 375 degrees. Wet a loaf of bread, lightly shaking off excess water. Cut bread lengthwise; place on sheet pan open side up. Drizzle olive oil generously over the bread; add fresh pepper to taste. Add Romano cheese, generously followed by anchovies in strips over cheese, if desired. Bake for 10 minutes or until cheese starts to turn golden brown; cut into 2-inch slices and enjoy with a glass of wine.

Sour Dough Bread

Recipe from Rose Lambi

2 cups of sponge (proofed starter)
2 Tbl. olive oil or softened butter
3 cups of unbleached all-purpose flour
4 tsp. sugar
2 tsp. salt

Place sponge in large mixing bowl; add sugar, salt and oil or softened butter; mix wel. Add flour 1/2 cup at a time; the flour is approximate measure and depends on the wetness of the sponge. Knead in enough flour to make a flexible bread dough.

Let the dough rest in warm place with a towel covered loosely over bowl. Sourdough rises slower than yeast breads; let dough double in size (approximately 1 hour); when a finger poked into the top of the dough creates a pit that doesn't spring back, you are ready to proceed.

Punch dough down and knead a few times; form dough into a loaf and place on baking sheet. Place in warm place with towel on top and let loaf double in size.

Place the pan with the loaf of bread in non-preheated oven then turn oven to 350 degrees; bake for approximately 30 to 45 minutes. Bread is done when the crust is brown and the bottom sounds hollow when thumped with a wooden spoon; turn loaf onto a cooling rack or towel and let cool for an hour before slicing.

Sour Dough Starter

Recipe from Rose Lambi

**1 cup warm water
1 cup unbleached bread flour**

Select a large jar or container to keep your starter; any wide-mouthed container will do—just **make sure metallic containers or utensils are NOT used**. For the first 3 to 7 days or more, leave in a warm place 70 to 80 degrees (100 degrees will kill it, so make sure the temperature is not too hot) and feed the starter every 24 hours by throwing half the starter away and adding the remaining starter with 1/2 cup flour and 1/2 cup warm water. When your proofed starter develops a bubbly froth, it is done and then can be refrigerated.

Once proofed and refrigerated, with lid on container, put a nail hole in the lid to give it breathing room and feed it weekly thereafter. You may develop "Hooch," which is a layer of watery liquid (often dark) that contains alcohol; it smells a bit like beer. Just pour it off or stir it back into starter; depending if your starter needs moisture or not. If you are going to use the starter for a recipe (sponge), then skip the feeding and continue with proofing the sponge.

To proof the sponge for baking, take the starter out of refrigerator, pour into a large glass or plastic bowl. Meanwhile, clean out your refrigerator container; add 1 cup warm water and 1 cup flour; stir well and keep in warm place for several hours (usually 6 to 8 hours. When your sponge is bubbly and has a white froth and smells sour, it is ready (the longer it sits, the more sour the flavor, so this is your preference). Measure amount needed for recipe and place leftover in cleaned refrigerator container, starting the process again.

Note: Can substitute all-purpose or wheat flour, but best results are obtained from unbleached bread flour.

Italian Bread

Recipe from Rose Lambi

1-1/2 cup lukewarm water
1 pkg. dry active yeast
4 cups flour
2 tsp. salt
1 Tbl. sugar

Dissolve yeast in lukewarm water in a small bowl; add dissolved yeast to other ingredients. Knead dough until dough is smooth; let rise 1 hour; punch down and shape. Cut slits on top of the bread; grease pan with olive oil; place into bread pan; let rise 30 minutes. Bake at 400 degrees for 40 to 45 minutes.

Makes 1 loaf

Cookies

1 cup buttermilk = 1 cup yogurt

1 cup milk = 1/2 cup evaporated milk + 1/2 cup water

1 cup sour milk = 1/2 milk + 1 Tbsp. lemon juice or vinegar

1 cup cake or pastry flour = 1 cup all-purpose less 2 Tbsp.

1 tsp. baking powder = 1/4 tsp. baking soda + 1/2 tsp. cream of tartar

1 cup sugar = 1 cup honey (use 1/4 cup less liquid in recipe)

1 cup brown sugar = 1 cup granulated sugar

1 cup oil = 1/2 lb. butter or margarine

1 Tbsp. prepared mustard = 1 tsp. dry mustard

1 clove garlic = 1/8 tsp. garlic powder

Emergency Substitutions

1 square chocolate = 3 Tbsp. cocoa + 1 Tbsp. butter

1 Tbsp. cornstarch (for thickening) = 2 Tbsp. flour

Anise Cookies

Recipe from Rose Lambi

1 cup shortening
3 eggs
1-1/2 cup sugar
1-1/2 tsp. baking powder
6 cup flour
1 Tbl. vanilla extract
3/4 tsp. crushed anise seed
1 tsp. anise oil

Cream shortening and eggs; add sugar, baking powder, flour, vanilla, anise seed and anise oil. Blend together until smooth and dough leaves the bowl clean. Divide dough into thirds; roll out and cut into strips; shape strips into rings. Bake at 350 degrees for 8 to 10 minutes.

Prepare glaze of 1-1/2 cup powdered sugar, water and 1/2 tsp. anise extract or oil. Add 1 tablespoon of water at a time; stir until you have a drizzle consistency. If desired, add food color to glaze; ice cookies when they are cooled. Make sure icing is completely dry on cookies before storing in containers.

Makes approximately 6 dozen cookies.

Anise Puffs

Recipe from Rose Lambi

2 cups all-purpose flour, sifted
1/8 tsp salt
3 eggs, separated
2-1/4 cups powdered sugar
1/4 tsp. anise oil

Sift flour and salt together, set aside. Beat egg whites until stiff peaks form when beaters are raised. Beat egg yolks until thick; fold into beaten egg whites. Gradually add sugar and continue beating on medium for 20 minutes; beat in dry ingredients and anise oil.

Drop by teaspoon 2 inches apart onto grease cookie sheet; let stand at room temperature uncovered for 4 to 8 hours. Bake in 350 degree oven for 10 to 12 minutes.

Makes 5 dozen cookies.

Crocanti (Peanut Cookie)

Recipe from Rose Lambi

3 cups sugar
3 cups flour, sifted
1 tsp. baking powder
1 lb. peanuts, chopped fine
3 Tbl. shortening, melted
2 tsp. vanilla extract
2 egg whites, beaten stiff

Mix sugar, flour, baking powder and peanuts in large bowl; add melted shortening and vanilla; fold in stiff egg whites. Add small amount water to moisten dough as a catalyst to hold dough together. Take half of dough, place on board and roll dough into 1-inch thick strings; cut strings into 1/2-inch pieces. Place on cookie sheet; bake at 375 degrees for about 10 minutes, until golden brown.

Cucidati (Fig Cookie)

Recipe from Dawn Wilson

Filling
1 lb. dried figs, chopped
1 cup seedless raisins
Rind of 1 large orange
1/2 lb. roasted walnuts,
chopped
1 tsp. cinnamon
1/2 cup bourbon whiskey
1 cup honey

Icing
1½ cups powdered sugar
Multi-colored cake sprinkles
Juice from 1 lemon

Pastry
2-1/2 cups flour
1/2 cup sugar
2-1/2 tsp. baking powder
1/4 tsp. salt
1 tsp. vanilla extract
1/4 cup milk
2 eggs slightly beaten
1/2 cup shortening

Preheat oven to 400 degrees.

For the filling: Grind figs, raisins, orange rind and nuts; stir in honey, whiskey and cinnamon.

For the pastry: Sift flour, sugar, baking powder and salt together; cut in shortening with pastry blender until the mixture resembles course corn meal; stir in eggs, milk and vanilla; mix until dough is soft; form pastry into ball; roll on a lightly floured surface to a ¼ inch thick; cut dough into 4-inch strips; spread a row of filling 1 inch thick on ½ of each strip; fold dough over to cover filling; press edges together to seal; cut into 1 inch slices; repeat until finished; place cookies on greased baking sheets 1 inch apart; bake until golden, 15 to 20 minutes; cool
on wire rack.

For the icing: Blend confectioner's sugar with lemon juice until smooth; glaze cookies with icing and decorate with cake sprinkles.

Momma Maria's Cucidati Cookie (Fig Cookie)

Recipe from Rose Lambi

Filling
1 lb. Calimyrna figs
1 lb. golden raisins
1/2 cup citrus candied fruit
1 lb. dates   1 large orange
1 to 2 cups honey
12 oz. mini chocolate chip morsels
1 lb. pecans
1 handful of sesame seeds (optional)

Grind all filling ingredients except chocolate chips, honey and sesame seeds; add chocolate chips and sesame seeds, mixing well while adding honey to ingredients.

Cookie Dough
6 cups flour
2 Tbl. baking powder
2 cups sugar
2 cups Crisco shortening
5 eggs, beaten
2 tsp. vanilla

Icing
1-1/2 cups powdered sugar
Drop of lemon,
orange or anise extract
Food color

Blend sugar and extract, and keep adding 1 tablespoon water at a time to form a consistency to drizzle icing over cookies. Add a drop of red or green food color to the icing, drizzle over cookie then add cake sprinkles, if desired.

Mix flour & baking powder; cut in shortening to make dough crumbly. Combine sugar, eggs and vanilla; add to flour mixture.

Roll out a small portion of cookie dough on floured board (I use a small juice glass to form a small circle); place fig in center of dough. Fold dough over to cover the fig mixture and pinch ends so mixture is not exposed. Place on ungreased cookie sheet and bake for 350 degrees until golden brown.

After cookies cool, place newspaper or wax paper on icing area; place cooling racks on top of paper and put cookies on cooling racks to ice them. Make sure icing is thoroughly dried before storing them in containers.

Italian Chocolate Spice Cookies

Recipe from Rose Lambi

3/4 tsp. baking powder	1 cup shortening
3/4 tsp. cloves	2/3 cup sugar
1/2 cup brewed coffee	2 Tbl. cocoa
2-1/2 cup flour	1 egg
1/2 cup uncooked peanuts	1/2 tsp. salt

Beat shortening, egg, cocoa and sugar together; add salt, baking powder, cloves, coffee and flour. Combine well, then add peanuts; roll into balls about the size of large marbles and bake at 350 degrees for about 12 to 15 minutes. Make a glaze of powdered sugar, almond extract and enough water to make the glaze; dip into glaze while holding bottom edge of cookie. Dry thoroughly on wire cooling rack before storing.

Glaze
1-1/2 cups powdered sugar
Drop of almond extract
Drop of red or green food color
Tablespoon of water at a time to make glaze

Makes about 4-1/2 to 5 dozen cookies.

Italian Drop Cookies

Recipe from Mary Midiri

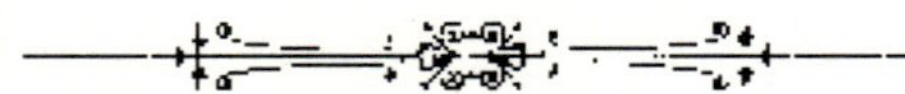

4 cups sifted flour
4 tsp. baking powder
1 cup sugar
3 eggs, well beaten
2 tsp. vanilla extract
1 cup milk
1 cup shortening
Pinch of salt

Cream shortening with sugar; add eggs and beat well; add baking powder with flour and salt; add milk and vanilla; drop by teaspoon onto greased cookie sheet; bake at 350 degrees for 10 minutes.

Note: If desired, raisins, nuts, cherries, or chocolate chips can be added to mixture before baking.

Icing
1 box powdered sugar
4 Tbl. butter or margarine
1 tsp. vanilla extract
Milk

Blend first three ingredients together and add milk to desired thickness; spread over cookies.

Mom's Italian Seed Cookies

Recipe from Mary Midiri

4 cups flour
1 Tbl. baking powder
1 cup shortening
3 eggs, beaten
1 tsp. vanilla
1/2 tsp. orange
1/2 tsp. lemon
Drop of anise oil
1 cup sugar
Milk, for moistening cookies
1 lb. sesame seeds

Mix flour and baking powder together; add shortening and mix with flour mixture. Mix eggs, flavorings and sugar together, then add to flour mixture; mix until dough is pliable. Take small amount on slightly floured cutting board and roll dough into ropes the size of a pencil; moisten rope with milk then roll into a line of sesame seeds. Cut into 1- to 1-1/2-inch sizes and place on cookie sheet, leaving about 1/8 inch between each cookie. Bake at 375 degrees for 10 to 12 minutes or until golden brown

Macaroon Magnifico

Recipe from Rose Lambi

2-2/3 cups flaked coconut
2/3 cup sugar
1/4 cup all-purpose flour
1/4 tsp. salt
4 egg whites
2 tsp. almond extract
1 cup chopped almonds
18 marischino cherries, halved

Mix coconut, sugar, flour and salt in mixing bowl; stir in egg whites and extract; stir in almonds; mix well.

Drop by teaspoonful onto lightly greased baking sheet; garnish with candied cherry halves, if desired. Bake at 325 degrees for 20 to 25 minutes, or until edges of cookies are golden brown; remove from baking sheet immediately.

Makes approximately 2-1/2 to 3 dozen.

Mini Biscotti Cookies

Recipe from Mary Midiri

5 cups all-purpose flour
1/2 tsp. salt
4 tsp. baking powder
1 cup shortening or butter
3 eggs, beaten
1 cup sugar
1/3 cup milk
1 tsp. vanilla
1 pkg. mini chocolate chips
Powdered sugar

Mix flour, salt and baking powder in large mixing bowl; add shortening and work together. Mix eggs, sugar, milk and extract together, and mix with flour mixture; add mini chocolate chips, mix well; knead a few times. Make cookies into 2-inch finger-shape size and place on baking sheet; bake at 350 degrees for 10 to 12 minutes or until light brown. When cool, sprinkle with powdered sugar.

Makes 4 dozen.

Aunt Virg's Nighty Nites

Recipe from Rose Lambi

2 egg whites, beaten stiff
2/3 cup sugar, add gradually to stiff egg whites
1/2 tsp. vanilla, add to above mixtures
Then add:
1 cup chopped pecans
1 cup chocolate chips

Drop by teaspoon on greased cookie sheet 1-inch apart; put in preheated 350 degree oven for 1 minute. Turn oven off and let Nighty Nites stay in oven overnight. DO NOT OPEN OVEN FOR 8 HOURS.

Makes 4 dozen.

When we lose, I eat. When we win, I eat. I also eat when it's rained out.

—Tommy Lasorda

Pecan Balls from Momma

Recipe from Rose Lambi

1 cup butter, softened
1/4 cup sugar
2 tsp. vanilla extract
2 cups flour
1-1/2 cups chopped pecans
3/4 tsp. salt
Powdered sugar

Cream butter, sugar and vanilla; add remaining ingredients, except powdered sugar and mix well. Form into small balls and chill for 1 hour in refrigerator. Bake at 300 degrees for 20 to 25 minutes; roll into powdered sugar while warm.

I am not a glutton—I am an explorer of food.
—Erma Bombeck

Press and Cut-Out Cookies from Momma

Recipe from Rose Lambi and Mary Midiri

4 cups flour
1 Tbl. baking powder
1 cup sugar
1 cup shortening
3 eggs
1 tsp. vanilla extract
Add milk, if necessary

Mix flour and baking powder; cream sugar, shortening, eggs and extract. Add dry ingredients; work together until pliable. Add a few drops of milk if necessary.

If using for press cookies, add a few drops of food color and decorate press cookie, to your desire.

If using for cut-out cookies, roll to 1/4-inch on a lightly floured board. Cut out cookies; bake, then decorate.

Bake at 400 degrees for 8 to 10 minutes.

Rose's Ultimate Chocolate Chip Cookie

Recipe by Rose Lambi

5 cups blended oatmeal	1 tsp. salt
2 cups butter	2 tsp. baking powder
2 cups brown sugar	2 tsp. baking soda
2 cups sugar	24 oz. chocolate chips
4 eggs	7 oz. Hershey Bar, cut into chunk-size pieces
2 tsp. vanilla	3 cups chopped nuts (your choice)
4 cups flour	

Measure oatmeal, and blend in a blender to a fine powder; cream the butter and both sugars; add eggs and vanilla, mix together with flour, oatmeal, salt, baking powder, and soda; add chocolate chips, chopped candy bar, and nuts; roll into balls, and place 2 inches apart on a cookie sheet.

Note: Recipe can be halved. (I do a full recipe, roll into balls and freeze in a single layer with 2 to 3 dozen cookies in each freezer bag.) Thaw a bag for 24 hours in refrigerator or quick thaw on counter for 1 hour; fresh, hot cookies with no mess!

Bake for 10 minutes at 375 degrees. (Do not overbake.)

Makes 112 large cookies or 192 small cookies.

Santa's Whiskers

Recipe from Mary Midiri

1 cup butter
1 cup sugar
2 Tbl. milk
1 tsp. vanilla
2-1/2 cups flour
1/2 cup chopped red and green candied cherries
1/2 cup chopped pecans
3/4 cup flaked coconut

Cream butter and sugar; blend in milk and vanilla. Stir in the flour, then cherries and pecans. Form dough into two 8-inch rolls; roll each in flaked coconut to coat outside. Wrap in wax paper and chill several hours or overnight; cut rolls into 1/4- inch slices; place on ungreased cookie sheet and bake at 350 degrees for 12 to 14 minutes.

Yields 5 dozen.

Sliced Cookies

Recipe from Mary Midiri

6 eggs
4 cups flour
1 tsp. baking powder
1 cup sugar
1 cup vegetable oil
1 cup pecans, chopped
1 cup raisins
1 cup candied cherries
3 or 4 drops anise oil

Mix by hand, eggs, oil and sugar; add flour and baking powder. Add nuts, cherries, and raisins; make 3 equal loafs. Bake at 350 degrees until lightly brown. Cool; slice on angle and re-toast.

Mom's "S" Cookie

Recipe from Mary Midiri

5 lbs. flour
4 Tbl. baking powder
1 tsp. salt
2 lbs. sugar
2-1/4 lbs. shortening
6 large eggs, beaten
2 tsp. vanilla extract
1 tsp. lemon extract
1 tsp. orange extract

Mix baking soda, salt and flour well and blend in short ening. In a separate bowl, mix eggs, vanilla, and extracts. Add to dry ingredients; add drops of milk to make a soft-dough. Roll dough in shape of a thick pencil, approximately 3 to 4 inches long. Shape into a S-shape; bake at 375 degrees until slightly golden brown. When cooled, frost tops by drizzling frosting with a teaspoon over cookies placed on cooling rack (place wax paper on table below cooling rack to catch any frosting that misses cookies).

<u>Frosting</u>
2 cups powdered sugar
1 tsp. lemon extract

Add a few drops of water at a time; mix and continue to add drops of water until a smooth consistency that will drizzle off spoon. Add a drop of red food color (icing color will be a pastel pink), then glaze the cookies. Let dry thoroughly before storing in containers.

Spice Balls

Recipe from Mary Midiri

1 cup Crisco shortening
1-1/4 cups sugar
3 eggs
1/2 cup black coffee
1 cup sweet wine
1/2 cup honey
7 cups flour

6 tsp. baking powder
4 Tbl. cocoa
2 tsp. ground cloves
2 Tbl. ground all spice
2 Tbl. cinnamon
1 cup chopped pecans
1 pkg. chocolate chips

Cream shortening, sugar, eggs and coffee. Mix 1 cup sweet wine and 1/2 cup honey with creamed ingredients; mix sifted ingredients with creamed mixture, then add nuts and chocolate chips. Roll into balls the size of a walnut; bake at 350 degrees for 12 to 14 minutes.

Note: add milk if mixture is too dry.

When cookie is cool, frost by holding edge of cookie; dip top section in frosting and place cookies on cooling rack (place wax paper on table below cooling rack to catch any frosting that may drip down cookie).

<u>Frosting:</u>
2 cups powdered sugar
1 tsp. vanilla extract

Add a few drops of water at a time; mix and continue to add drops of water until you get a smooth consistency that will drizzle off the spoon. Add a drop of red *or* green food color (icing color will be a pastel color); glaze the cookies. Let dry thoroughly before storing in containers.

Walnut Crescents

Recipe from Dawn Wilson

**1 cup (2 sticks) unsalted butter, softened to room temperature
1-1/4 cup confectioner's sugar, divided
2 tsp. vanilla extract
1-1/2 cup water
2 cups all-purpose flour
1-1/4 tsp. salt
1 cup walnuts or pecans, finely chopped**

Heat over to 375. In medium bowl, with electric mixer on medium, beat butter and 1/4 cup confectioners sugar until creamy, about 1 minute. Add vanilla and water. With mixer on low, gradually add flour and salt, beating just until blended; stir in nuts with a wooden spoon. With lightly floured hands, roll dough into 1-1/4 inch balls; shape balls into crescents. Arrange 2 inches apart on ungreased baking sheet; bake 15 minutes or until lightly browned. Place remaining 1 cup confectioner's sugar in a medium bowl; while cookies are still warm, toss in confectioner's sugar to coat. Transfer cookies to wire racks to cool completely; toss cookies in sugar once more to double coat.

A man seldom thinks with more earnestness of anything than he does of his dinner.
—Samuel Johnson

Almond Cookies

Recipe from Rose Lambi

2-3/4 cups all-purpose flour
1 egg, beaten
1 cup sugar
2 tsp. milk
1 tsp. baking soda
1 cup butter, softened
1/2 tsp. salt
1 tsp. almond extract
48 blanched almonds

Mix flour, sugar, baking soda and salt; cut in butter until mixture resembles fine crumbs. Mix egg, milk and extract, then add to flour mixture. Mix well; shape dough into large marble-sized balls. Place 2 inches apart on cookie sheet; place almond in center of each cookie and press to flatten slightly.

Bake at 325 degrees for 20 minutes.

Makes 4 dozen.

Gooey Butter Cookies

Recipe from Betty Guccione

1/2 cup butter
1/4 tsp. vanilla extract
1 egg
1 8-oz. cream cheese
1 box butter recipe yellow cake mix
Powdered sugar
Pam spray

Beat butter, vanilla, egg, cream cheese until light and fluffy; mix in dry cake mix. Cover and chill 30 minutes; heat oven to 350 and spray Pam on cookie sheet. Drop dough by teaspoon in bowl of powdered sugar; roll into balls. Bake 12 to 16 minutes; when cool, sprinkle with powdered sugar.

A kitchen condenses the universe.
—Betty Fussell

Spice Cookies (Vola's recipe)

Recipe is dated 12/03/1984
Recipe from Dawn Wilson

1 lb. sweet butter
1 cups Wesson oil
2 cups sugar
1 cup orange juice, fresh
1 tsp. orange peel, graded
1 shot of Cognac
1/2 tsp. ground cloves
1/2 tsp. cinnamon
3 tsp. baking powder
1 tsp. baking soda
4 eggs
9 to 10 cups flour

Mix all ingredients. Roll into balls; bake at 350 degrees.

Italian Seed Cookie

Recipe from Gwen Guccione

1 cup sugar
2 eggs
1 tsp. vanilla extract
1 tsp. almond extract
1 cup shortening
3 cups flour
1 tsp. baking powder
1/4 tsp. salt
Sesame seeds

Cream sugar, eggs, extracts and shortening with a mixer; add flour, baking powder and salt. Take small amount of dough, roll in rope-style shape, then in sesame seeds. Cut into 2-inch pieces and bake at 350 degrees until golden.

The discovery of a new dish does more for the happiness of mankind than the discovery of a star.
—Anthelme Brillat-Savarin

DESSERTS

Helpful Hints

▲ The freshness of eggs can be tested by placing them in a large bowl of cold water; if they float, do not use them.

▲ Cracked eggs should only be used in dishes that are thoroughly cooked; they may contain bacteria.

▲ For a quick, low-fat crunchy topping for muffins, sprinkle the tops with Grape-Nuts cereal before baking.

▲ Dust a bread pan or work surface with flour more evenly by filling an empty glass salt shaker with flour.

▲ Egg whites need to be at room temperature for greater volume when whipped.

▲ Keep strawberries fresh for up to 10 days by refrigerating them (unwashed) in an airtight container between layers of paper towels.

▲ When decorating a cake with chocolate, you can make a quick decorating tube. Put chocolate in a heat-safe zipper-lock plastic bag. Immerse in simmering water until the chocolate is melted. Snip off the tip of one corner and squeeze the chocolate out of the bag.

▲ To get that silky, molten look that professionally decorated cakes have, frost your cake as usual, then use a hair dryer to blow-dry the surface until the frosting slightly melts.

Apple Nut Bread

Recipe from Rose Lambi

1/2 cup packed shredded carrots
1 cup sweetened applesauce
1/2 cup vegetable or corn oil
1 tsp. vanilla extract
2 eggs, beaten
3/4 cup granulated sugar

2 cups all-purpose flour
1 tsp. double acting baking powder
1/2 tsp. baking soda
1/2 tsp. salt
1 tsp. cinnamon
1/2 tsp. nutmeg
1/2 cup chopped walnuts

Combine carrots, applesauce, oil and vanilla in bowl; add eggs and sugar, mixing all ingredients together.

Mix dry ingredients and nuts together; stir into applesauce mixture; mix only until all ingredients are blended. DO NOT OVERMIX. Pour into greased and floured loaf pan; spread batter evenly and add toppping.

Topping:
5 Tbl. sugar
½ tsp. cinnamon

Combine sugar and cinnamon; sprinkle over batter; bake at 325 degrees for 1 hour or until a wooden pick inserted in center comes out clean; bread should have crack down center. Remove from pan and cool on wire rack. WOW!

Banana Bread

Recipe from Mary Midiri

1/2 cup (1 stick) butter
1 cup sugar
2 large eggs
1-1/2 cup flour
1 tsp. baking soda
1 tsp. salt
1 cup mashed bananas
1 tsp. vanilla extract
1/2 cup sour cream
1/2 cup pecans

Cream butter and sugar; add eggs. Mix flour, baking soda and salt; add to creamed mixture. Blend bananas, vanilla and sour cream; mix only to blend with butter mixture. Add 1/2 cup of pecans. Bake at 350 degrees for 1 hour and 10 minutes or until toothpick comes out clean.

Tina's Brownies

Recipe from Mary Midiri

4 squares unsweetened chocolate
2/3 cup Crisco shortening
2 cup sugar
4 eggs
1-1/2 cups flour
1 tsp. baking powder
1 tsp. salt
1 cup nuts

Melt the chocolate and shortening together; beat in sugar and eggs. Blend flour, baking powder and salt; fold in nuts. Place in a greased 9 x 13 pan and bake at 350 degrees about 30 minutes.

A smiling face is half the meal.
—Latvian proverb

Canolli Pudding

(Grandma Guccione's recipe)
Recipe from Dawn Wilson and Rose Lambi

3/4 cup cornstarch
1 cup sugar
3-1/2 cups milk
Chocolate, chopped or shaved
Maraschino cherries (for decoration)
1/2 teaspoon lemon extract

Mix all items except chocolate and cherries; cook over medium-high heat, stirring with a wooden spoon until just before boiling point. Lower heat and continue stirring until it thickens; remove from heat and let cool; stuff shells. Place 1/2 maraschino cherry on each end of canolli; sprinkle with powdered sugar.

Fills 12-15 canolli shells.

Canolli Ricotta Filling

Recipe from Rose Lambi

16 oz. Ricotta cheese
1 cup sifted powdered sugar
1 tsp. vanilla
1/2 cup mini chocolate morsels
1 tsp. cinnamon
1 cup heavy whipping cream

Beat Ricotta cheese at medium speed for 30 seconds; add sugar and vanilla, beat 1 to 2 minutes. Fold in chocolate & dash of cinnamon; whip heavy cream and add to mixture. Fill canolli shell and garnish end with 1/2 maraschino cherry. Sprinkle shell with powdered sugar or dip ends in chocolate sprinkles.

Recipe fills 12 to 15 shells.

Routine in cuisine is a crime.
—Edouard Nignon

Chocolate Eclair Squares

Recipe from Dawn Wilson

**2 small boxes vanilla pudding
9 oz. carton Cool Whip
1 lb. box graham crackers**

Butter bottom of 13 x 9 pan; cover with whole graham crackers. Prepare pudding according to directions and add Cool Whip; pour approximately half the mixture over graham crackers to cover. Add layer of graham crackers, remaining pudding and final layer of graham crackers.

**Topping:
2 oz. unsweetened chocolate
3 tsp. corn syrup
1 tsp. vanilla
3 Tbl. butter or margarine
3 Tbl. milk
2 cups powdered sugar**

Cook everything until melted, then add sugar; blend well. Pour over crackers; refrigerate uncovered for 2 days.

Note: You can double the topping to create a thicker topping, if desired.

Cassata

Recipe from Rose Lambi

6 cinnamon sticks
1/2 gallon whole milk
1 cup cornstarch
1-1/2 cup sugar
1 pound cake (store-bought or homemade)
10 maraschino cherries, stemless, halved
1/2 lb. chocolate, chopped

Simmer the cinnamon sticks in half the milk for approximately 20 minutes; DO NOT BOIL; sift the cornstarch before measuring; mix with the sugar. Add and mix the remaining milk and stir well. Strain cinnamon sticks from simmered milk and add milk to the other milk mixture. Cook together until thickened over low/medium flame; stir constantly using WOODEN SPOON only.

Once thickened, ladle mixture in 13 X 9 glass dish. Place 1 layer of thinly sliced pound cake; then half of the remaining cream mixture, followed by half of chocolate, then another layer of thinly sliced pound cake. Add the rest of the cream mixture; decorate the top with cherries and rest of chocolate.

Prepare 1 day ahead of time (after 1 hour in refrigerator, cover loosely with waxed paper) and keep refrigerated until ready to serve.

Mary's Cream Puff Cake

Recipe from Rose Lambi & Mary Midiri

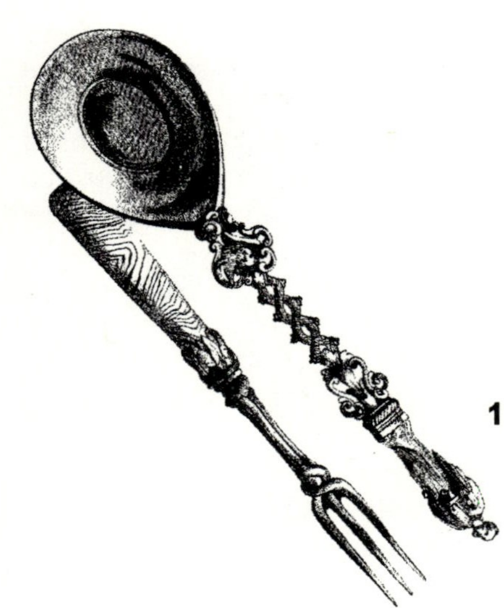

1 cup water
1/2 cup butter
1 cup flour
4 eggs
1 large and small package instant vanilla pudding
3 cups milk
12 oz. cream cheese, softened
12 oz. Cool Whip
Chopped nuts and chocolate syrup

Crust: In saucepan boil 1 cup water and butter, bring to a bubble; remove from stove; add flour mixing with WOODEN spoon; add eggs 1 at a time, mix well; spread on jelly roll pan or glass lasagna-sized pan; bake at 400 degrees for 30 minutes; cool crust.

Filling: Add together pudding and milk and mix with electric mixer according to directions; add cream cheese and mix until smooth; spread over crust; spread Cool Whip; add chopped nuts and drizzle chocolate over cake prior to serving, if desired.

Note: Do not drizzle chocolate ahead of time as it will bleed into Cool Whip.   Serves 16.

Crunchy Caramel Apple Pie

Recipe from Rose Lambi

Pie Ingredients:

6 cups thinly sliced peeled & cored Golden delicious or
Fuji apples
1 9-inch pastry crust for a deep-dish pie
1/2 cup sugar
3 Tbl. all-purpose flour
1 tsp. ground cinnamon
1/8 tsp. salt
Crumb topping (recipe to right)
1/2 cup chopped pecans
1/4 cup caramel topping

Crumb Topping:

1 cup packed brown sugar
1/2 cup all-purpose flour
1/2 cup quick cooking rolled oats
1/2 cup butter

Directions for Crumb Topping:

Stir together brown sugar, flour, rolled oats; cut in 1/2 cup butter until topping is like course crumbs; set aside.

Directions for Pie:

In a large bowl, stir together the sugar, flour, cinnamon and salt. Add apple slices and gently toss until coated; transfer all into pie shell. Sprinkle crumb topping over apple mixture; place pie on a cookie sheet or aluminum foil to avoid dripping from dropping on oven. Cover piecrust edge with aluminum foil; bake in pre-heated 375 degree oven for 25 minutes. Remove foil from pie crust edge and bake for an additional 25 to 30 minutes. Remove from oven; sprinkle with chopped pecans and then drizzle with caramel topping. Cool on wire rack and enjoy warm or at room temperature.

Death by Chocolate

Recipe from Dawn Wilson

1 brownie mix (for a 13 x 9 pan)
1 large box of instant chocolate pudding or
chocolate mousse
16 oz. Cool Whip
6-8 Heath or Skor candy bars, broken into small chunks
1 cup or more Kahlua Liquor

Prepare brownie mix as directed: bake in 13 x 9 pan; let cool for approximately 15 minutes. Poke holes in brownie top with a fork; drizzle Kahlua on top of brownies so that it soaks into the holes; divide brownies in half.

In a large glass bowl, layer half the brownies, half the pudding, half the Cool Whip and half the candy bars; repeat process, topping with candy bars. Cover and refrigerate for 24 hours before serving.

Fudge by Uncle Sam

Recipe from Rose Lambi

3/4 stick butter
1 cup milk
3 cup sugar
1 tsp. vanilla extract
12 oz. chocolate chips
7 oz. marshmallow cream
1 cup nuts, chopped

Cook butter, milk, and sugar over medium high heat on a double boiler until a soft bubble forms; add vanilla, chocolate chips & marshmallow cream in specific order given. Stir in nuts; place in a glass 13 X 9 pan; let cool and form before cutting into 1" squares.

Heavenly Hash from Aunt Virg

Recipe from Rose Lambi

1/2 cup (1 stick) butter or margarine
12 oz. chocolate chips
1 can Eagle Brand milk
2 cups miniature marshmallows
1 cup nuts

Melt butter or margarine and chocolate chips; mix in Eagle Brand milk then the remaining ingredients. Place in lightly greased 13 X 9 pan until set; cut into small squares. Great-looking when served on a holiday cookie tray.

Man is the only animal, I believe, who pretends he is thinking of other things when he is eating.
—*Robert Lynd*

Italian Lemon Ice (Granita)

Recipe from Rose Lambi

4 cups water
1 cup granulated sugar
1/4 cup fresh lemon juice
Finely grated zest (yellow part of rind of 1 lemon)

Bring water & sugar to boil, and simmer over moderate heat until sugar is completely dissolved. Let cool slightly, then refrigerate until cold.

In bowl, mix syrup, lemon zest and lemon juice; freeze until ice crystals form around the edges (about 30 minutes). Stir well, return to freezer, and stir every 30 minutes until granita is frozen (about 2-1/2 hours).

Italian Spingi (Italian Doughnuts)

4 cups water
4 cups sifted flour
1 dozen eggs, beaten
12 Tbl. shortening
12 Tbl. sugar
OR
12 Tbl. cinnamon with pecan pieces

Heat water until hot, but not boiling. Add flour and cook until very dry; remove from heat and add beaten eggs (1/4 volume at a time) and mix with wooden spoon. Heat shortening over medium high heat and drop by tablespoon into hot oil and fry until golden brown. Drain on paper towel; eat warm or cool with honey poured over the doughnuts and sprinkle with sugar, cinnamon or chopped nuts (whichever you prefer).

Light Dessert

Recipe from Mary Midiri

6 oz. sugar-free Jello
1 small can crushed pineapple
1 small can mandarin oranges (drained)
24 oz. cottage cheese (fat free or 1%)
4 oz. lite Cool Whip

Mix together Jello and pineapple with juice until dissolved; add remaining ingredients and refrigerate.

Myra's New York-Style Cheesecake

Recipe from Dawn Wilson

Crust:
1-1/4 cups finely ground almonds
OR
1-1/4 cups finely ground cashews
Sweetener equal to 1 Tbl. sugar
6 Tbl. butter, melted

Topping:
2 cups sour cream (16 oz. container)
1 tsp. vanilla extract
Sweetener equal to 1 Tbl. sugar

Filling:
3 pkg. (8 oz. each) cream cheese, softened
Sweetener equivalent to 1 cup sugar
4 eggs
1 tsp. vanilla extract

In a bowl, combine the almonds (or cashews), 1 tablespoon sweetener and melted butter until combined; press into bottom of a 9-inch springform pan. Chill in the refrigerator at least 15 minutes. In a bowl, mix the sour cream, 1 teaspoon vanilla and 1 tablespoon sweetener until well combined; cover with plastic wrap and refrigerate. In a large bowl, beat the cream cheese and 1 cup sweetener until fluffy; add the eggs, one at a time, blending well after each addition. Blend in the remaining 1 teaspoon vanilla.

Pour the cream cheese mixture into the springform pan, and bake at 350 degree for 50 minutes or until a knife inserted halfway between the edge and center comes clean. With a spatula, spread the sour cream mixture over the top, making sure you reach to the edges of the pan. Return cake to oven and bake an additional 5 minutes; remove cake from oven, allow to cool to room temperature (cake will settle in the pan). Slide a knife around the edge of the cake to loosen it, then remove the springform ring; keep chilled in the refrigerator.

Makes 16 servings, about 5 grams of carbs per serving if made with almonds, and 7.2 grams per serving if made with cashews.

Aunt Rose's Old-Fashioned Cheesecake

Recipe from Rose Lambi, Dawn Wilson & Mary Midiri

**1 can crescent rolls
3 pkgs. (8 oz. each) cream cheese, softened
5 eggs
1 cup sugar
1 cup (8 oz.) sour cream
2 tsp. vanilla extract**

Roll & pat crescent rolls in an ungreased 13 X 9 cake pan. Cream remaining ingredients, then pour cream mixture on top; sprinkle lightly with cinnamon. Bake at 350 degrees for 50 minutes.

Serves 12 to 16.

Whoever is of merry heart has a continual feast.
—*Proverbs 15:15*

Ooey Gooey Butter Cake

Recipe from Dawn Wilson

**1/2 cup (1 stick) butter, melted
1 egg, beaten
1 box of yellow cake mix**

Mix the above ingredients and spread into a greased 9 x 13 pan.

**2 eggs
8 oz. cream cheese
1 lb. powdered sugar**

Beat above ingredients for 3 to 5 minutes; pour over the mixture that is already in the 9 x 13 pan. Bake at 350 degrees for 30 to 40 minutes or until golden brown.

Serves 8 to 10.

Pinulata

Recipe from Rose Lambi

1 Tbl. sugar
1/2 tsp. salt
4 Tbl. butter
4 eggs
3 cups flour
Vegetable oil
Honey syrup (see right)
1/2 to 1 cup chocolate chunk pieces
1/2 cup slivered almonds

Honey Syrup:
3/4 cup honey
1/3 cup water
1/3 cup sugar

Cook for 15 minutes, stirring constantly.

Mix sugar, salt, butter and eggs in bowl; add flour (1 cup at a time). Let mixture set for at least 1/2 hour. Divide dough into 10 pieces; roll each piece into a rope the thickness of a pencil; cut pieces about the size of a pencil eraser. Fry pieces in hot oil, stirring to keep each piece separated. Remove with a serrated spoon and drain on paper towels.

Make honey syrup and pour over fried nougats; add pieces of chocolate and almonds and shape in a cone-shape on a decorative plate; sprinkle with decorate sprinkles, if desired.

Toffee Ice Cream Dessert

Recipe from Rose Lambi

3 cups cream-filled chocolate sandwich cookie crumbs
2 cups butter or margarine, melted
1/2 gallon vanilla ice cream, softened
1 (7.5 oz.) pkg. almond brickle chips
Fudge sauce, heated
Whipped topping
Maraschino cherries

Combine cookie crumbs and butter, stirring with a fork; press firmly into bottom of a lightly greased 13 X 9 inch baking dish; bake at 350 degrees for 5 minutes; let cool.

Spread half of ice cream over crust; sprinkle with half of brickle chips; repeat layers; cover and freeze until firm; cut into squares to serve; top each serving with fudge sauce, a dollop of whipped topping and a cherry.

Note: This is an ideal supper club dessert. You can make it ahead, it serves a crowd, and the ingredients can't miss.

Makes 15 to 18 servings.

Tiramisu

Recipe from Rose Lambi

1-1/2 cups milk; reserve 1/4 cup
1/2 cup granulated sugar
4 large egg yolks
2 Tbl. cornstarch
2 Tbl. unsalted butter, divided
2 tsp. vanilla extract

2 Tbl. light rum
1/2 lb. Mascarpone cheese, at room temperature
1-1/4 cups cold brewed espresso
2 Tbl. coffee liqueur
24 Italian Savolardi cookies
2 squares semi-sweet chocolate, grated

In saucepan over medium heat, scald 1-1/4 cup milk with the sugar, stirring until dissolved. In 1-quart glass measure, whisk remaining 1/4 cup milk, the yolks and cornstarch until smooth. Whisk a little milk mixture into yolk mixture; whisk in remaining milk mixture. Return to saucepan; bring to a boil, whisking. Continue to boil, whisking for 2 minutes until thickened. Strain through fine mesh sieve into clean bowl; whisk in butter, rum and vanilla until blended. Place plastic wrap directly on surface of custard to prevent skin from forming and refrigerate until chilled (about 2 hours).

Remove from refrigerator; fold in mascarpone. Beat heavy cream until stiff peaks form; fold into custard. To assemble, in small bowl, mix espresso and liqueur. Dip 12 ladyfingers (1 at a time) into espresso mixture until some liquid is absorbed; arrange in 9 X 9 inch square glass baking dish or 2-quart casserole, side by side, in 2 rows of 6 to cover bottom (if using 8-inch dish, push ladyfingers together to fit); spread half the custard evenly on top; sprinkle with half the grated chocolate; dip remaining ladyfingers (one at a time in espresso mixture); form second layer, as above. Spread remaining custard on top; sprinkle with remaining grated chocolate. Cover; refrigerate at least 8 hours or overnight.

To serve, cut into 9 squares. Place on dessert plates; dust with confectioners' sugar. Top with grated chocolate and raspberries, if desired.   Serves 9.

Substitutions:
- Use strong coffee instead of espresso.
- If mascarpone cheese is unavailable, combine 2 tablespoons milk, 3/4 cup ricotta cheese, 2 tablespoons softened cream cheese and 3/4 teaspoon lemon juice in blender or food processor; puree until smooth.
- If using sponge ladyfingers instead of Savolardi cookies (crisp ladyfingers), do not separate into individual ladyfingers; let strips sit uncovered at room temperature overnight to become stale. Use 1 package (2 strips) plus 3 single ladyfingers for each layer.

Williamsburg Bread

Recipe by Rose Lambi

2 pkg. crescent rolls
2 pkg. cream cheese
1-1/2 cup sugar, 1/2 cup reserved
1 egg
1 tsp. vanilla
2 tsp. cinnamon

Spread 1 can crescent rolls in shallow pan, pressing seams together. Mix 2 pkg. cream cheese (8 oz each), 1 cup sugar, 1 egg yolk (reserve white for top of crust), and 1 teaspoon vanilla. Spread mixture on top of crescent roll; top with can of crescent rolls, then brush with beaten egg white. Sprinkle with a mixture of 1/2 cup sugar and 1/2 teaspoon cinnamon.

Bake at 375 degrees for 30 minutes.

Cut into squares and serve warm.

Serves 6-8.

Aunt Virg's Zucchini Bread

Recipe from Rose Lambi

2 eggs
3 cups flour
1 cup vegetable oil
1 tsp. salt
2 tsp. vanilla extract
1 tsp. baking soda
2 cups zucchini, grated
1/2 tsp. baking powder
2 cups sugar
1 cup pecans or walnuts, chopped

Grease and flour 2 loaf pans. Beat eggs, add oil, sugar, zucchini and vanilla; mix together well. Add dry ingredients to mixture; beat well. Add nuts, mixing by hand. Bake 1 hour at 350 degrees.

Makes 2 loaves.

Zucchini Pineapple Bread
by Teresa McVey

Recipe from Dawn Wilson

3 eggs
2 cups sugar
2 tsp. vanilla extract
2 cups zucchini
1 cup oil
3 cups flour
1 tsp. baking soda
1 tsp. salt
1 tsp. baking powder
1 cup crushed pineapple
1/2 cup raisins
1 cup pecan pieces

Beat eggs until fluffy; add sugar, vanilla, oil and zucchini; blend well. Add dry ingredients and mix well; stir in pineapple, raisins and nuts. Bake in 2 small floured and greased bread pans at 325 degrees for 50 to 60 minutes.

Serves 8.

Canolli Shells

(Grandma Guccione's recipe)
Recipe from Dawn Wilson

2 cups flour
1 tsp. cinnamon
1/4 cup sugar
1/2 tsp. salt
3 Tbl. whiskey
2 eggs
3 Tbl. shortening

Rub shortening into ingredients; roll out dough unto a well-floured board; cut in circles to about a 5-inch circumference. Form circles on a canolli form or wooden dowel 6 inches long and 1/2-inch circumference; pinch with milk. Deep fry until golden brown; store in tin containers to keep fresh.

Peach Pie á la Dawn

Recipe from Dawn Wilson

3/4 cup flour
1 tsp. baking powder
1/2 tsp. salt
1 egg
1/2 cup milk
3 Tbl. margarine, softened
1 pkg. (2.9 oz.) vanilla pudding, cook and serve
29 oz. can of sliced peaches, drained; reserving the juice
8 oz. cream cheese
1/2 cup sugar
1/2 tsp. ground cinnamon

Mix together flour, baking powder, salt, egg, milk, margarine and pudding in mixing bowl. Beat 2 minutes at medium speed with electric mixer; pour into greased 9-inch pan. Arrange peach slices over pudding layer; beat together cream cheese, 1/2 cup sugar and 3 tablespoons reserved peach juice. Spoon cream cheese layer over peaches, leaving 1-inch rim around outside. Combine 1 tablespoon sugar and cinnamon and sprinkle over cream cheese. Bake in preheated oven at 350 degrees for 30 to 35 minutes or until golden brown; store in refrigerator.

Strawberry Angel Food Dessert

Recipe from Mary Midiri

**1 Angel Food Cake (store bought or homemade), cut
into bite-sized pieces
1 large box strawberry Jello, dissolved with 2 cups
boiling water
2 tsp. lemon juice
1 large bag frozen strawberries, thawed and sliced
1 large container Cool Whip
1 cup (8 oz.) sour cream**

Place pieces of cake in 9 X 13 pan; dissolve Jello in large bowl; cool. Add lemon juice and sliced strawberries. Add Cool Whip and sour cream to Jello mixture; mix and pour over cake. Refrigerate.

One cannot think well, love well, sleep well, if one has not dined well.

—*Virginia Woolf*

Chocolate Turtle Cake from Aunt Virg

Recipe from Rose Lambi

**1 box Swiss or German chocolate cake mix
1 bag (14 oz.) caramels
1/2 cup Pet milk
3/4 cup margarine
1 cup chocolate chips
1 cup pecan pieces**

Mix cake mix according to directions; pour half of batter in greased and floured 13 X 9 cake pan and bake until done. While cake is baking, melt caramels, Pet milk and margarine in medium saucepan over medium heat, stirring constantly until caramels are melted; add chocolate chips and pecans to melted caramel mixture. Use a spatula to evenly distribute over cooked cake; add rest of cake mix and bake 20 to 25 minutes longer. Serve warm or at room temperature.

ENTREES

Helpful Hints

▲ To cut down on odors when cooking cabbage, cauliflower, etc., add a little vinegar to the cooking water.

▲ To avoid tears when cutting onions, try cutting them under cold running water or briefly placing them in the freezer before cutting.

▲ Perk up soggy lettuce by soaking it in a mixture of lemon juice and cold water.

▲ Vinegar can remove spots caused by tomatoes. Soak the spot with vinegar and wash as usual.

▲ To keep hot oil from splattering, sprinkle a little salt or flour in the pan before frying.

▲ A few drops of lemon juice added to simmering rice will keep the grains separated.

▲ To dress up buttered, cooked vegetables, sprinkle them with toasted sesame seeds, toasted chopped nuts, canned french-fried onions, or slightly crushed seasoned croutons.

▲ A little vinegar or lemon juice added to potatoes before draining will make them extra white when mashed.

▲ To quickly bake potatoes, place them in boiling water for 10 to 15 minutes. Pierce their skins with a fork and bake in a preheated oven.

Basil Shrimp

Recipe from Rose Lambi

1/4 cup butter, melted
2-1/2 Tbl. olive oil
Juice of 1-1/2 lemons
3 Tbl. Dijon-style prepared mustard
1 bunch fresh basil, stems removed
3 cloves garlic, minced
Salt and white pepper
3 lb. shrimp, peeled and de-veined

In shallow bowl add olive oil to melted butter; then add lemon juice, mustard, basil, garlic, salt and pepper. Mix well, then add shrimp and toss to coat; cover and refrigerate for 1 hour.

Preheat grill to high heat; lightly oil grate. Remove shrimp from marinade and thread on skewers; place skewers on heated grill and cook about 2 minutes on each side. This is a must-try recipe; best I have ever eaten.

Note: If using wooden skewers, soak in water for 1 hour to prevent them from burning on the grill.

Serves 4.

Beef Scalloppine Marsala

Recipe from Rose Lambi

1 cup long grain rice, cooked
10 oz. pkg frozen peas, thawed
3 lb. beef top round steaks, each cut 1/4-inch thick
1 egg, beaten with 3 Tbl. milk
1-1/4 cup bread crumbs
1/4 cup Parmesan cheese, grated
1 tsp. salt
1/8 tsp. pepper

1/2 cup (1 stick) & 5 Tbl. butter
1 garlic clove, whole
3/4 cup water
2 tsp. all-purpose flour
1/2 cup Marsala wine
1/4 cup minced parsley
1 beef bouillon cube

Cook rice according to directions; add peas; keep warm. Pound each steak to 1/8-inch thickness; then cut into 4 X 2 inch pieces. In shallow pan, beat egg with milk; in second shallow pan, combine bread crumbs, Parmesan cheese, salt and pepper. Dip meat in egg mixture, then in bread crumb mixture.

In large skillet over medium high heat, melt 2 tablespoons butter. Cook garlic and 1/4 of meat until meat is lightly browned. Remove to platter keeping warm; repeat with remaining meat and butter, using 1/2 cup butter (1 stick) in all.

In cup mix water with flour; discard garlic from skillet and melt remaining 5 tablespoons of butter. Add water mixture, wine, parsley and bouillon cube. Cook stirring until thickened, pour over meat; serve with rice and peas.

Serves 6-8.

Beef Spedini

Recipe from Rose Lambi

3 lbs. Spedini meat
1/4 cup vegetable or Canola oil
2 cups Italian seasoned bread crumbs
2 cups very small cubed celery, sautéed in butter
Prosciuto ham, diced very small
2 cups grated Parmesan

1 cup chopped onion
1 cup roped provel cheese, diced small
1 can whole or diced tomatoes, (cut into pieces if whole)
1 medium onion, quartered
Bay leaves

Mix all ingredients except meat and tomatoes, quartered onions and bay leaves; separate meat and let each piece fall as it may in medium bowl. Pour oil in bowl and move meat around to get all meat moistened with oil; take each piece and dip in bread crumb mixture and lay flat. Add 1 tablespoon of ingredient evenly over meat; add 1 teaspoon of tomatoes on top of mixture on meat, then roll meat like a jelly roll. Place on a skewer, placing an onion slice and bay leaf between each spedini. Spray grill with oil and brown on each side of spedini (approximately 3 minutes on each side) and serve.

Note: You can make spedinis ahead and refrigerate up to 2 days in advance or freeze (omit the quartered onions and bay leaves if freezing) if not being cooked within 2 days. These were a well-kept Italian secret until recently, but now are being served in some Italian restaurants. Our parents served Spedini with "Garlic Lemon Sauce," found in the *Soup, Salad and Dressing* section, brushed on top of Spedini after grilling.

Beef Spedini (Mary Midiri's recipe)

Recipe from Dawn Wilson

2 Tbl. garlic, minced
3 cups vegetable oil
3 cups breadcrumbs, seasoned
1 cup Parmesan cheese
3 Tbl. parsley
14-1/2 oz. can tomatoes, diced
1/4 pound Provel cheese, cut into strips
1 eye of round steak, cut into thin steaks similar to breakfast steaks
2 tsp. garlic salt
15 bay leaves, broken into pieces
1 onion, quartered and separated
1/4 cup lemon juice

Slice meat thinly; marinade steaks in oil with minced garlic overnight in refrigerator, covered. Mix breadcrumbs, parsley, Parmesan cheese, pepper and garlic salt; dip steaks into this mixture and coat well. Lay meat flat and layer with tomato and cheese; roll up tightly and stick on a skewer. Put onion and bay leaf between meat rolls; broil or barbeque, approximately 5 minutes then turn and continue cooking until golden brown. Baste with lemon and garlic sauce while grilling.

Note: You may substitute chicken or turkey cutlets instead of beef.

Blue Cheese Meatloaf

Recipe from Rose Lambi

1-1/2 lbs. ground beef
1/2 lb. ground pork
2 cups plain breadcrumbs
1-1/2 Tbl. Dijon mustard
1/2 cup milk
2 eggs, beaten
2 Tbl. parsley
1/2 cup onion, minced
1/4 cup ketchup
4 ounces blue cheese, crumbled

Combine all ingredients in a mixing bowl and mix well. Place in a lightly oiled loaf pan; bake at 350 degrees for 60 to 75 minutes. This is a nice twist to an old favorite.

Serves 4 to 6.

Breakfast Pizza

Recipe from Mary Midiri

1 lb. sausage
1 green pepper, diced
1 small onion, diced
1-1/2 lb. hash browns
1 cup milk
16 oz. egg beater
Salt and pepper

Brown green pepper and onions with sausage. Put in casserole dish; top with hash browns. Mix egg beaters, milk and salt and pepper; pour over hash browns; top with cheddar cheese. Bake for 30 minutes at 350 degrees.

I hate people who are not serious about their meals.
—Oscar Wilde

Brozzaloni

Recipe from Rose Lambi

2 round steaks, 1/4-inch thick
2 cups Italian bread crumbs
1 cup Romano cheese
1 tsp. salt
1/2 tsp. pepper
12 slices Provolone cheese

12 thin slices Italian salami (optional)
4 hard-cooked eggs, quartered
1/2 cup parsley
Waxed paper & kitchen string
1/4 cup olive oil

Lay round steaks on wax paper (if bone-in remove and crimp surrounding meat together to hide hole); mix bread crumbs, Romano cheese, salt and pepper; spread bread crumb mixture evenly over both steaks to within 1/2 " to the edge of meat; next place 6 slices salami and 6 slices provolone cheese on each steak, then eggs, followed by parsley.

Begin to roll the steak away from you jellyroll style, keeping the filling inside of meat; once rolled place toothpicks to hold roll; tie up one end with string and continue to wrap string around roll about an inch apart until the end and tie off and cut end of string; in a sauté pan, sear all sides of meat in hot oil; prepare your favorite spaghetti sauce and cook in sauce for approximately 45 minutes to 1 hour; remove from sauce, let cool completely then cut in ½ inch thick slices and place on flat serving plate; when ready to serve, microwave to warm meat then serve with a side dish of pasta and salad.

Serves 6 to 8

Chicken Anthony

Recipe from Rose Lambi

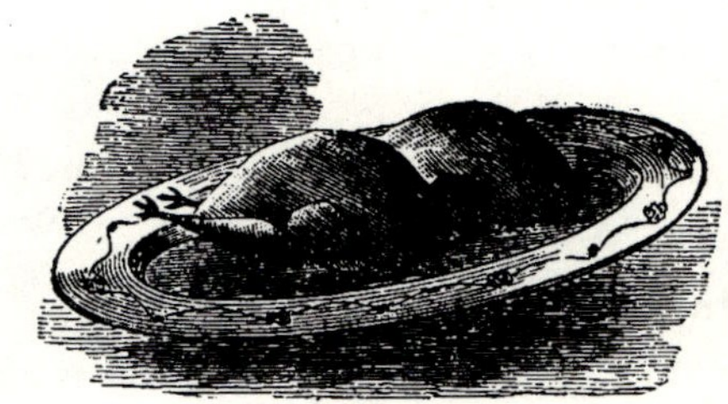

8 chicken breasts, boneless and skinless
1/2 cup flour
1 egg
1/2 cup milk
1 to 2 cups Italian breadcrumbs
1/4 cup olive oil
8 oz. chicken broth
1 cup sliced mushrooms
1 large head of broccoli, prepared into spears
1 clove garlic, chopped
8 slices Provel cheese

Pound chicken to make uniform thickness; dip in flour, then in egg wash (egg and milk), then in Italian breadcrumbs. Sauté in olive oil in large skillet until golden brown; remove chicken and place in baking dish. Place chicken broth, mushrooms, garlic and broccoli in skillet and heat thoroughly, stirring in drippings from skillet. Pour over chicken then place 1 slice of Provel cheese over each chicken breast. Cook in 350 degree oven for 30 minutes or until tender.

Serves 8.

Chicken con Artichoke

Recipe from Rose Lambi

4 chicken breast, skinned and boneless
Salt and pepper, to taste
Paprika
6 Tbl. butter, divided
1 can (15 oz.) artichoke hearts
4 to 6 oz. mushrooms, sliced
4 green onion, chopped
2 Tbl. flour
1 cup chicken broth
1/4 cup red cooking wine
1/2 tsp. rosemary, crushed

Season chicken with salt, pepper and paprika; in a large skillet, melt 3 tablespoons butter over medium high heat. Add chicken and fry until brown on all sides. Transfer to a 2-quart casserole; arrange artichoke hearts between the chicken. Add remaining butter to skillet stirring in drippings and adding mushrooms and green onions; sauté until tender. Sprinkle flour over mushrooms; stir in chicken broth, wine and rosemary; cook mixture, stirring constantly for 3 to 5 minutes. Pour over the chicken and bake covered for 40 minutes at 375 degrees. Serve over rice or pasta.

Serves 4.

Chicken Daniel

Recipe from Rose Lambi

4 chicken breasts, boneless and skinless
1 cup milk
2 eggs
2/3 cup all-purpose flour
1 cup Italian seasoned breadcrumbs
3 Tbl. vegetable oil
3 cups Half-and-Half

10 oz. Provel cheese rope (about 2½ cups)
1/4 tsp. garlic powder
1 tsp. salt
1/2 tsp. coarsely ground pepper
4 cups fresh mushrooms, sliced
20 broccoli florets, blanched and drained
2 cups Parmesan cheese

Preheat oven to 375 degrees.

With a meat mallet, lightly pound the thicker end of each breast half to make pieces uniform in thickness. In a medium bowl, beat together milk and egg. Place flour in pie pan and bread crumbs in another pie pan; dip chicken in egg mixture, then coat with flour; dip back into egg mixture, then cover with bread crumbs.

Heat an ovenproof skillet over medium-high heat; add oil and chicken; fry until golden brown (about 2 minutes on each side). Place skillet in oven; bake 12 to 14 minutes to an internal temperature of 175 degrees.

Meanwhile in a medium saucepan, combine Half-and-Half, Provel, garlic powder, salt and pepper; turn heat to medium. When Provel melts, add mushrooms and broccoli; cook 3 to 5 minutes; stir in Parmesan and increase heat to high; boil until sauce thickens. (If sauce is too thick, add Half-and-Half; if sauce is too thin, add more cheese.) Ladle over chicken and serve.

Serves 4.

Chicken Maria

Recipe from Rose Lambi

2 cups chicken stock
1/4 tsp. garlic, chopped
1 tsp. lemon juice
1/3 cup sherry wine
1/2 cup (1 stick) butter
4 Tbl. flour

1-1/2 cups shredded Provel cheese
1/2 tsp. cracked black pepper
1 cup lump crabmeat
4 chicken breasts, boneless and skinless
12 asparagus spears
2 cups mushrooms, sliced

Bring chicken stock, garlic, lemon juice and sherry wine to a boil. In small saucepan melt butter; when butter is melted, add flour to make a roux. Add roux to boiling ingredients, stirring constantly; reduce heat to low. Add shredded cheese, black pepper, mushrooms and crabmeat.

Salt and pepper chicken breasts, dredge in flour and sauté in skillet with 3 tablespoons oil over medium high heat. Cook asparagus while chicken is sautéing.

Place chicken breast on platter, lay 3 asparagus spears on top of each breast and ladle sauce over top of each chicken serving.

Serves 4.

Chicken Marsala

Recipe from Rose Lambi

4 boneless, skinless chicken breasts
1/4 cup all-purpose flour
1/2 tsp. salt
1/2 tsp. pepper
3 Tbl. vegetable oil
1 cup chicken broth
1/4 cup Marsala wine
1 clove garlic, minced
1/4 lb. portabella mushrooms, sliced
2 green onions, thinly sliced

Pound chicken breasts between sheets of waxed paper to 1/2-inch thickness; on another sheet of waxed paper, combine flour, salt and pepper; dredge chicken in flour mixture. In large skillet, heat oil over medium heat; fry chicken breasts 3 to 4 minutes per side, or until tender; remove from skillet; keep warm.

In same skillet, combine broth, wine, garlic, mushrooms and onions; increase heat to high; bring mixture to a boil; reduce heat to medium; simmer mixture 3 to 4 minutes, stirring occasionally; return chicken to pan; cook 2 to 3 minutes, or until chicken is heated through; serve immediately.
Serves 4.

Filet Oscar

Recipe from Rose Lambi

2 beef filets (8 oz each)
8 asparagus spears, steamed
3 oz. crab meat
2 egg yolks
2 tsp. lemon juice
Dash Tabasco sauce
6 oz. butter, melted
1/4 cup white wine vinegar
1 tsp. tarragon

Whip the egg yolk in a metal mixing bowl; add the lemon juice and Tabasco. Place over steaming water; heat stirring constantly, for 1 minute. Remove from the heat and slowly whisk in the butter, stirring constantly. Add the vinegar and tarragon to a small skillet; boil until almost dry; add to the sauce and set aside.

Grill the steaks to the desired temperature. Trim the asparagus tips to the size of the steaks; place on top of the steaks. Garnish with the crabmeat and the sauce; serve warm.

Serves 2.

Jim's Ham Glaze

Recipe from Mary Midiri

2 heaping Tbl. concentrated frozen orange juice
1 lb. brown sugar
2 shots of whiskey
Diced orange rind

Score and put whole cloves in ham where you scored it; combine ingredients and simmer until thick; spoon on ham periodically while baking.

Italian Hamburgers

Recipe from Rose Lambi

2 lb. ground beef
3 eggs
1/4 cup chopped fresh parsley
1 cup Italian bread crumbs
3/4 cup Parmesan cheese, grated
2 tsp. ground garlic, fresh
3/4 to 1 cup water
Salt and pepper, to taste
Medium onion, sliced thin
1 green pepper, sliced thin
Large loaf French bread

Mix ground beef, eggs, parsley, breadcrumbs, Parmesan cheese, garlic and water; salt and pepper to taste. Shape hamburgers to fit French bread sliced into 6" sandwiches. Sauté in large skillet over medium to medium high heat, turning when golden brown on first side. Garnish with onion and pepper and serve with your favorite condiments.

Serves 4.

Italian Meat Balls

Recipe from Rose Lambi

**2 lb. ground chuck
1 cup plain bread crumbs
1 cup Parmesan cheese, grated
3 cloves garlic, finely chopped
1/4 cup scallions, chopped
1 cup water
3 to 4 eggs
1 tsp. pepper
1-1/2 tsp. salt
1/4 cup parsley, finely chopped**

Mix all ingredients in large bowl. Form meat balls approximately 1-1/2 inch in diameter; dip fingertips in oil to make forming meat balls easier. Sauté in large skillet until golden brown, rotating to brown all sides of meat balls. Place in your favorite spaghetti sauce and cook an additional 30 minutes.

"Mock" Veal Cutlets

Recipe from Rose Lambi

**1 pork tenderloin, whole
1 large egg, beaten with 1/4 cup water
1 cup Italian breadcrumbs
3/4 cup Parmesan cheese
1/4 cup vegetable or canola oil**

Cut tenderloin into 1" fillets; with a meat mallet, pound each fillet to 1/8" thickness. Dip in egg mixture, then in breadcrumb mixture; sauté in large skillet over medium heat for approximately 3 minutes on each side until golden brown. Serve with lemon wedge, or you can make your favorite wine-cheese sauce poured over cutlets. No one will know the difference between these cutlets and your more expensive veal cutlets.

Serves 4 to 6.

Mussels Steamed in Tomato-Wine Sauce

Recipe from Rose Lambi

2 Tbl. butter
1 small onion, finely chopped
2 cloves garlic, finely chopped
1 can (14-1/2 oz.) Italian tomatoes
1/8 tsp. crushed dried red pepper
2 lb. mussels, well-scrubbed
1/2 cup parsley, finely chopped
1/2 cup dry white wine

Melt butter in large skillet on medium; add onion and garlic; cook, stirring occasionally, until onions are soft (about 5 minutes). Add tomatoes and pepper flakes; cover and reduce heat; simmer 15 minutes. Increase heat, add mussels, parsley and wine; cover and bring to a boil. Reduce heat again and simmer until shells open, about 7 to 10 minutes.

Mussels are cooked when shells open to reveal orange flesh inside; discard any mussels that do not open. Serve at once with thick slices of Italian bread.

Serves 2 entrees or 4 appetizers.

Steak or Chicken Modiga

Recipe from Rose Lambi

4 Chicken breasts, skinless & boneless,
pounded to 1/8 inch thickness _or_
4 rib eye steaks, 3/4 to 1 inch thick
1/4 to 1/2 cup vegetable oil
1 cup Italian breadcrumbs
1 cup Parmesan cheese
1 tsp. heavy ground pepper
1 tsp. garlic salt

Sauce:
4 Tbl. flour
1/2 cup butter
1-1/2 cup Provel cheese
2 cups chicken broth
1/4 tsp. garlic
1 Tbl. lemon juice
1/2 cup white dry wine
1/2 tsp. coarsely ground pepper
2 cups sliced fresh mushrooms

Modiga: Dip meat in oil, then in mixture of breadcrumb, Parmesan cheese, salt and pepper; grill approximately 6 to 8 minutes on each side (spray grill prior to placing meat on it to avoid sticking). If unable to grill, place in skillet with small amount of oil and sauté on each side to a golden brown; remove from heat and keep warm.

Sauce: In a large skillet, bring chicken broth, garlic, lemon juice and wine to a boil. Meanwhile, melt butter in a small saucepan. When melted, add flour to butter to make a roux. Add roux to chicken broth mixture, stirring constantly; reduce heat to low; add shredded Provel, black pepper and mushrooms; ladle sauce on cooked modiga.

Note: Can use the Garlic Lemon Sauce Recipe found in _Soup, Salad and Dressing_ section instead of the sauce recipe included in this recipe.

Veal or Chicken Picata

Recipe from Rose Lambi

4 Chicken breasts or 8 slices veal
(approximately 1 to 1-1/2 pounds)
2 to 3 Tbl. flour
1 tsp. salt
1/2 tsp. paprika
4 Tbl. olive oil
1/4 cup fresh parsley, chopped
1 lemon sliced
1 Tbl. lemon juice

4 Tbl. butter
1/2 cup dry white wine
1/3 cup chicken broth
3 cloves garlic
1 medium shallot, chopped
6 oz. mushrooms, sliced thin
2 oz. capers

Dredge chicken or veal in mixture of flour, salt and paprika. In large skillet, heat oil over medium high heat; add lemon slices in pan for 1 minute, remove and set lemon slices aside. Place veal or chicken in pan and brown on both sides; remove to a platter and keep warm. Do NOT clean skillet. Melt 1 tablespoon butter in skillet and cook shallots in medium heat for approximately 2 minutes; pour in wine, parsley, mushrooms and broth and bring to a boil over high heat, scraping any drippings into the sauce with a wooden spoon. Boil until reduced by half in volume; stir in lemon juice and remaining butter. Add capers at the end and ladle over chicken or veal.

Serves 4.

Veal Saltimbocca

Recipe from Rose Lambi

1 lb. thin sliced veal cutlets
1/4 lb. thin sliced proschiutto
1/2 lb. Provel cheese
1-1/2 cup chicken broth
1/2 cup white dry wine

1 tsp. lemon juice
1/2 tsp. rubbed sage
4 Tbls. flour
1/2 cup butter
1/2 tsp. cracked black pepper

Sauce: Bring to a boil chicken stock, wine, lemon juice and sage. In another saucepan, melt butter, add flour to make a roux; add roux to boiling stock stirring constantly. Reduce heat to low and add black pepper.

Veal: Salt and pepper veal, dredge in flour and sauté. Arrange veal in ovenproof baking dish or sauté pan; top veal with prosciutto slices and Provel cheese. Ladle sauce over veal and bake in a hot oven at 450 degrees, just long enough to melt cheese and heat thoroughly.

Note: For a more economical version, use pork tenderloin. Slice 1-inch thick pieces and pound to thin cutlets.
Serves 4.

Every man should eat and drink and enjoy the good of all his labor; it is the gift of God.
—Ecclesiastes 3:13

Veal Saltimbocca (pocket style)

Recipe from Rose Lambi

4 large slices of veal, pounded 1/8 inch thick
2 thin slices of Prosciutto, halved
1/2 tsp. dry sage
4 tsp. Parmesan cheese, grated
1/2 cup beef broth
1 egg beaten with 3 Tbl. water

1 cup flour
6 Tbl. butter, divided
1/4 cup Marsala wine
1/4 cup white wine, dry
Salt and pepper

Lay veal flat on waxed paper; place prosciutto equally over half of each slice of meat; divide the cheese and sage evenly the same 1/2 slice of meat; take the 1/2 slice of meat without the Prosciutto, sage and cheese and fold over the section with the Prosciutto, sage and cheese. Place in refrigerator for 10 minutes. In a shallow pan, beat egg with water. In another bowl, combine the flour and 1 teaspoon salt. Melt 2 tablespoons butter in large skillet over medium high heat; dip each veal package first into the egg, then the flour. Sauté until brown on the bottom. Add another tablespoon of butter to the pan; turn the veal and brown on second side; remove from skillet and keep warm.

Add the Marsala and white wine to the pan, and reduce over high heat until 1/8 cup remains; add remaining butter and beef broth; lower the heat to medium and whisk until the butter is melted into the sauce; season with salt and pepper; spoon the sauce over the veal and serve immediately.

Note: Mock veal can be used in place of veal, just make your fillets larger than direction on mock veal in order to make larger slices.

Serves 4.

Beef Filet with Mushrooms in Wine Sauce

Recipe from Rose Lambi

**3 Tbl. butter or margarine, divided
1-1/2 lb filet mignon or tenderloin tip cut into ½" strips
3 shallots or 1 small red onion, finely chopped
1 lb fresh mushrooms sliced
1/2 cup port or Marsala wine
Salt and pepper, to taste
1 pkg. (10 oz) Pepperidge Farm frozen Puff Pastry
Shells, baked according to directions**

In a large skillet, sauté meat in 1 tablespoon butter until pink. Remove meat and set aside. Heat 1 tablespoon butter in skillet, add shallots and mushrooms and sauté until golden brown. Add wine; increase heat while stirring. Reduce to half the volume; add remaining butter and stir quickly into mixture. Serve immediately in warm pastry shells.

Serves 6.

Bella's Favorite Chicken

Recipe from Kerrie Sheeley

**4 large chicken breasts
3 cups breadcrumbs
1-1/2 cups Parmesan-Romano Cheese
1 Tbl. garlic salt & 1/2 Tbl pepper
1/2 cup vegetable oil
8 oz. package mushrooms
4 Tbl. butter**

Mix breadcrumbs and cheese together in bowl; salt and pepper chicken breast then dip in oil, then in the breadcrumb mixture. Place in a pan or baking sheet and bake at 350 degrees for 1 hour. Prior to chicken being cooked, melt butter in medium saucepan and sauté mushrooms; serve over chicken for a great quick dinner.

Chicken a´la Rosa

Recipe from Rose Lambi

6 chicken breast, boneless and skinless
1/4 cup white wine
1 can cream of chicken soup, undiluted
6 slices Swiss cheese
1/3 cup butter
2 cup herb stuffing mix, crushed

Mix wine and soup; place chicken breasts in baking dish; pour soup and wine mixture over chicken. Cover each chicken breast with a slice of Swiss cheese. Melt butter and mix with stuffing mix; cover chicken with buttered stuffing mix.

Bake at 350 degrees for 1 hour or until chicken is tender. Your guests will think you have been slaving in the kitchen all day!

Serves 6.

Chicken Dijon

Recipe from Rose Lambi

4 chicken breasts, boneless and skinless
1/2 cup flour
Dijon mustard
4 Tbl. butter
1/3 cup white wine
1 cup whipping cream

Pound chicken breast until even thickness; put flour in shallow pan or plate. Spread Dijon on 1 side of breast; put side with mustard in flour; spread mustard on other side of breast and dip in flour. Melt butter in skillet over medium high heat; brown breast well on each side (approximately 5 minutes per side); remove and keep warm.

Add 1/3 cup white wine to skillet, mixing dripping with wine; bring to a boil. Add 1 cup whipping cream and 2 tablespoons Dijon mustard. Stir 5 to 7 minutes until sauce thickens; lower heat, adding chicken, and simmer for 5 minutes.

Serves 4.

Easy Chicken Supreme

Recipe from Rose Lambi

4 chicken breasts, boneless & skinless
1/2 cup dry white wine
1/2 cup Parmesan cheese
1/2 cup Italian breadcrumbs
Salt and pepper to taste
Pinch of ground nutmeg

Spray a square 8-inch casserole with cooking spray; place breasts in casserole. Add wine; sprinkle lightly with salt, pepper and nutmeg. Mix cheese and breadcrumbs together and sprinkle evenly over the top.

Bake uncovered at 375 degrees for 25 to 30 minutes, until chicken is done and topping is browned.

Serves 4.

Creamy Scallops and Mushrooms

Recipe from Rose Lambi

1/2 lb. fresh mushrooms, sliced
1 medium onion, sliced
1 lb. scallops
1/3 cup dry sherry
4 Tbl. butter, divided
1/4 cup all-purpose flour
1 cup Half-and-Half
1/2 tsp. salt
Pasta or rice, cooked according to directions

Sauté mushrooms and onions in 1 tablespoon butter until tender; add scallops and sherry, bring to a boil. Reduce heat and simmer, uncovered, 8 minutes, stirring occasionally. Melt 3 tablespoons butter in a medium saucepan over low heat; add flour, stirring until smooth. Cook 1 minute; add Half-and-Half, stirring constantly until mixture is thickened and bubbly. Stir in salt; add sauce to scallops, stirring gently, cook, uncovered, just until heated. Serve over pasta or rice.

Serves 4.

Shrimp Scampi

Recipe from Rose Lambi

1 lb. shrimp, cleaned
4 to 6 cloves garlic, chopped
4 Tbl. butter
1 Tbl. lemon juice
1/2 tsp. salt
3 Tbl. parsley flakes

Sauté shrimp, garlic in butter until shrimp are 3/4 cooked. Add lemon juice, salt and parsley flakes. Serve with your favorite side dish of pasta and vegetable.

Dining is and always was a great artistic opportunity.
—Frank Lloyd Wright

PASTA

and RICE

Enlivening Leftovers

▲ Enliven leftover rice by adding bacon bits, peas, chopped bell peppers, onions, celery, or other veggies. Heat some oil in a skillet; add the rice and stir over medium heat until hot. For a quick lunch, add one or two eggs mixed with soy sauce.

▲ Break leftover cake into pieces; layer with softened ice cream. Freeze, then slice to serve.

▲ Leftover cheese can be melted with skim milk to make a sauce for vegetables or noodles or to use as a cheese dip. Use a heavy pot and low heat; stir constantly.

▲ Add leftover cooked vegetables to salad or sandwhich spreads or arrange on top of lettuce and add dressing.

▲ Save leftover spaghetti sauce in small plastic freezer bags. Thaw in the microwave and add to hot noodles when needed.

▲ Brown leftover potatoes with onion and egg for a light supper. Top with diced bell peppers and salsa.

▲ Leftover mashed potatoes can be flavored with cheese and fried in patties for a side dish or breakfast.

▲ Make vegetable hash by combining leftover corn, bell peppers, potatoes, peas, and beans with onion, garlic, and other seasonings.

▲ Garlic bread can be frozen and then grated to make a coating for chicken, chops, and vegetables.

Canneloni Stuffing

Recipe from Rose Lambi

8 oz. chicken
8 oz. veal
4 oz. chopped spinach, cooked & drained
8 oz. mushrooms, chopped very fine
1 cup Parmesan cheese
4 Tbl. (1/2 stick) butter
2 eggs
Water or chicken broth
Favorite spaghetti sauce
2 cups Mozzarella cheese

Boil chicken and veal in water or chicken broth. When cooked, remove meat & reserve broth; finely grind meats & finely chop spinach. Add meats and spinach together. Sauté mushrooms in butter; add mushrooms and cheese to mixture. Add 1 egg at a time (both may not be needed); if dry with both eggs, add reserve broth. Stuff mixture in a very al dente cannelloni noodle; place on a 13 X 9 pan, placing your favorite sauce on bottom of pan prior to placing stuffed canneloni. Finish with sauce and mozzarella cheese on top and bake for 30 minutes at 350 degrees.

Serves 6 to 8.

Couscous with Fresh Tomato and Basil

Recipe from Dawn Wilson

1 lemon peel finely grated
1 Tbl. lemon juice
1 Tbl. olive oil
2 plum tomatoes, finely diced
2 Tbl. basil, slivered
1/4 tsp. pepper
1 cup couscous
2 cups water
1/4 tsp. salt
1 tsp. garlic, chopped

Combine lemon peel, lemon juice, olive oil, tomatoes, basil and pepper; set aside. In a medium saucepan, combine couscous, water, salt and garlic; bring to a boil, stirring well. When at a steady boil, remove from the heat; cover and set aside for 5 minutes; stir in tomato mixture and serve.

Fettuccini Sauce

Recipe from Rose Lambi

1/2 cup (1 stick) butter
2 cloves garlic, crushed
1 cup mushrooms
1/4 cup fresh parsley, diced
Half-and-Half cream
1 cup Parmesan cheese

Bring ingredients to a boil; simmer 5 minutes. Serve over fettuccini or any other pasta noodle. To make sauce thinner, add additional Half-and-Half; to make sauce thicker add additional cheese.

Note: Add clams or shrimp, if desired.

The problem with eating Italian food is that five or six days later you're hungry again.
—George Miller

Garlic Butter Sauce with Angel Hair Pasta

Recipe from Rose Lambi

5 cloves garlic, minced
1/4 cup olive oil
1/2 cup (1 stick) butter
1/2 cup fresh parsley, minced
Grated Parmesan cheese
1 lb. Angel Hair pasta, cooked to directions

Cook garlic over medium low heat with butter and olive oil until just turning golden; stir in parsley and cook another 1-1/2 minutes. Pour over cooked pasta; toss to coat pasta and serve with Parmesan cheese.

Serves 2 to 4.

Green Rice

Recipe from Mary Midiri

4 cups cooked rice
1 large bag frozen chopped broccoli
1 small onion, chopped
1 cup milk
1/2 cup vegetable oil
1 lb. Velvetta cheese, cubed

Mix all ingredients in large mixing bowl and put in a greased 9 x 13 pan; bake for 1 hour at 350 degrees.

Serenely full, the epicure would say,
Fate cannot harm me, I have dined today.
—Sydney Smith

Homemade Pasta

Recipe by Rose Lambi

**3 cup flour
2 tsp. salt
3 eggs, beaten
2 Tbl. vegetable oil**

Pour flour on a working surface and make a well in the center. Add salt, egg and mix in well; work dough together while gradually adding oil until dough becomes shiny & elastic-like. Roll out very thin and cut into strips or use a pasta machine if you have one; let dry for 1 hour. Add to boiling water for a few minutes; check for your preferred doneness.

Note: Homemade pasta cooks faster than store-bought boxed pasta.

Linguini and Clams

Recipe from Jo Merklin

**1 lb. of Linguini pasta
2 Tbl. garlic, chopped
1 cup fresh parsley, chopped
2 large cans clams
1 bottle clam juice
3/4 cup olive oil
4 to 6 oz. Parmesan cheese**

Prepare Linguini according to package directions. In large skillet heat oil, garlic and parsley; add clams and clam juice. When pasta is cooked, drain and add to garlic parsley mixture; heat thoroughly and top with Parmesan cheese.

When a man's stomach is full it makes no difference whether he is rich or poor.
—Euripides

Lasagna

Recipe from Rose Lambi

1 lb. Lasagna pasta
1 Tbl. vegetable oil
32 oz. Mozzarella cheese, shredded
16 oz. Parmesan cheese, shredded

16 oz. Ricotta cheese
4 Tbl. parsley flakes
1 egg
Meat sauce (see page 97)

Make a large batch of Meat Sauce (see separate recipe).

Cook lasagna in boiling salted water until partially cooked (still hard but slightly flexible). While lasagna is cooking, mix ricotta cheese, parsley and egg in small bowl. Drain hot water from lasagna, rinse with cold water; then, add cold water to cover lasagna with 1 tablespoon vegetable oil to avoid lasagna from sticking to each other.

Begin layering lasagna in this order: Spaghetti sauce on bottom of pan, noodles, spaghetti sauce, small dollop ricotta cheese mixture on 4 to 5 areas per layer, 1/4to 1/2 bag of mozzarella cheese, sprinkle well with Parmesan cheese, then start another layer beginning with lasagna pasta; keep layering until you have used all the lasagna noodles.

Prepare pan. Lasagna can be left in refrigerator for 3 to 4 days (glass pan only or disposable aluminum pan) before baking, or you can freeze if consumption will be at a later time. Bake at 350 degrees for 30 to 45 minutes, removing the foil the last 20 minutes of baking; wait 10 to 15 minutes after removing from oven before cutting.

A pan yields 12 to 15 slices of lasagna.

Linguini Pescatore

Recipe from Rose Lambi

1 lb. linguini, cooked very al dente
1 cup (2 sticks) butter
6 oz. mushrooms, sliced
1/2 cup fresh parsley, chopped
2 Tbl. garlic, chopped
2 cups fish stock or chicken broth
1 lb. medium shrimp, peeled & de-veined
3/4 cup clams, chopped
6 oz. crabmeat, drained and flaked (about 2/3 cup)
Salt and pepper, to taste
Parmesan cheese, grated

Cook linguini according to package directions, but stop when linguini is about 3/4 cooked; pour into colander and drain. In same pan used for cooking pasta, melt butter; add mushrooms, parsley, garlic and fish stock or chicken broth. Bring to a boil; add shrimp. Return to boiling; reduce heat and simmer 3 to 4 minutes or until shrimp are almost done. Add pasta, clams and crabmeat to mixture in pan; cook until mixture is heated thoroughly and pasta and shrimp are done. Serve with Parmesan cheese.

Serves 4 to 6.

Low Carb Spaghetti

Recipe from Rose Lambi

1 large or 2 small spaghetti squash
1/4 cup olive oil
1 medium onion, chopped
2 cloves garlic, chopped
1 large eggplant, 1/2-inch cubes
1 lb. medium shrimp, peeled and de-veined

1 lb. medium scallops
10 green or black olives, sliced or chopped
1 cup mushrooms, sliced
1 tsp. basil or 5 fresh leaves, chopped
6 plum tomatoes, chopped
1 cup cooking wine

Take spaghetti squash, cut lengthwise in half and place open side down in 350 degree oven for 30 minutes. While squash is baking, take large skillet over medium high heat and sauté onions in olive oil for 5 to 7 minutes, then add garlic and eggplant. Continue cooking for 5 minutes; add shrimp, scallops and olives for another five minutes, followed by the remaining ingredients. Let all simmer for 5 minutes or until the juices from the tomatoes begin to flow; add wine.

Let squash cool for a few minutes, then take each section of squash and with a fork, scrape with a top to bottom motion the inside of squash, which will cause the squash to have the appearance of spaghetti; pour ingredients in skillet over squash, sprinkle with Parmesan cheese. This is a great way to supplement your craving for pasta when you are watching calories and carbs.

Serves 4.

Manicotti from Momma (Italian Crepes)

Recipe from Rose Lambi

Your favorite Italian spaghetti sauce
Manicotti (crepes):
6 eggs
1/4 tsp. salt
1-3/4 cup water
1-1/2 cup unsifted flour

Filling:
4 oz. can sliced black olives
2 eggs
16 oz. ricotta cheese
1 tsp. salt
12 oz. shredded mozzarella cheese
1 Tbl. parsley flakes
1 cup grated Parmesan cheese
Parmesan cheese for sprinkling on top (1/3 cup)

Make manicotti batter by beating together flour, water, eggs and salt; set aside for 1/2 hour. Griddle thin crepes, each consisting of 3 tablespoon batter; mix all filling ingredients except Parmesan cheese. After manicotti crepes are made, stuff each crepe with 1/4 cup of filling; roll up and place close together in baking dish with sauce poured over and Parmesan sprinkled on top. Bake 1/2 hour at 350 degrees.

Orzo with Feta, Green Beans & Tomatoes

Recipe from Rose Lambi

10 oz. haricots verts (thin green beans)
1 medium onion, chopped
3 medium tomatoes, sliced into 1/4-inch strips
1 Tbl. white wine vinegar
1 cup crumbled feta cheese
1 cup orzo pasta (rice-shaped pasta)
2 garlic cloves, minced
2 Tbl. olive oil
1 Tbl. parsley leaves, chopped

Trim beans and cut into 1" pieces; in large skillet over medium heat, cook onion and garlic in olive oil until onion is soft. Add tomatoes and cook, stirring until tomatoes are softened, about 2 minutes; remove skillet from heat.

Have a bowl with ice and cold water ready. Place beans in salted boiling water, blanch beans 1 minutes. With a slotted spoon, transfer bean to ice water to stop cooking; then drain beans well and pat dry. Add beans to tomato mixture and return water to a boil. Cook orzo until firm and drain in colander; add orzo to bean mixture; add vinegar, parsley, feta, salt and pepper, tossing to combine well.

Serves 2.

Pasta Verde

Recipe from Rose Lambi

2 Tbl. Dijon mustard
2 Tbl. Sherry vinegar
1/4 cup + 2 Tbl. olive oil
Salt and pepper to taste
1/2 cup scallions, thinly sliced
2 small zucchini, halved lengthwise 1/4-inch thick
8 oz. snap peas, tough strings removed
3 oz. baby spinach, stems trimmed and coarsely chopped
1/4 cup packed fresh basil, cut into very thin strips
1 lb. cooked Gemelli or other short pasta

In medium bowl, whisk together mustard and vinegar; while whisking, slowly drizzle in 1/4 cup oil until emulsified. Season with salt and pepper; set aside. Cook pasta according to directions until al dente (about 8 minutes); drain, return to pot and set aside.

Meanwhile, heat remaining 2 tablespoons of oil in large skillet over medium heat; add scallions. Cook until translucent; add zucchini. Cook, stirring until tender, about 4 minutes; add snap peas and spinach. Cook, stirring until bright green, about 2 minutes. Remove from heat; stir in scallions and basil; add to pasta along with vinaigrette. Toss; serve warm.
Serves 4.

Pasta with Anchovy Sauce

Recipe from Mary Midiri

5 Tbl. olive oil
2 onions, finely chopped
12 to 14 canned anchovy fillets, chopped
1 Tbl. butter
1/2 cup milk
1 lb. Linguini pasta
1 cup flat-leafed parsley leaves, chopped

Place a large pot of salted water for pasta over high heat. Take a large heavy-based pan over medium heat and add olive oil; toss in onions. Reduce heat to low and sauté until soft. Add anchovies; stir in butter and 1 tablespoon water; gradually stir in milk; remove from heat. Cook pasta to directions; reserve 1/2 cup pasta water before draining pasta. Add pasta to anchovy sauce; mix in a bit of the pasta water; add 2/3 cups parsley and toss. Place pasta in bowls; garnish with parsley and serve.

Pasta in Garlic Sauce

Recipe from Jo Merklin

1 lb. Angel Hair pasta
1/4 cup olive oil
1/4 cup fresh parsley, chopped
4 cloves of garlic, finely chopped
1/4 cup freshly grated Parmesan cheese
Fresh ground pepper

Cook pasta as directed on package. Meanwhile, heat oil in skillet over medium-high heat; sauté parsley and garlic in oil, stirring frequently, until garlic is soft. Drain pasta; mix with garlic mixture; grate fresh pepper and cheese.

The last taste of sweets is sweetest last.
—William Shakespeare, Richard II

Pasta with Gorgonzola Cheese

1 lb spinach-flavored Linguini pasta
5 Tbl. unsalted butter, divided
4 oz. mushrooms, sliced
6 black olives, pitted and sliced
2 cups heavy cream
10 oz. Gorgonzola cheese
Salt and fresh-ground pepper to taste
1 Tbl. parsley, finely chopped
1/4 cup Parmesan cheese

In a small skillet, sauté 1 tablespoon butter with mushrooms and olives.

In a medium saucepan, reduce the cream over medium-high heat until 1-1/2 to 1-3/4 cups remain and cream has thickened; this will take 7 to 8 minutes. Crumble the gorgonzola cheese into the cream and stir until it is completely melted in; do not boil once the cheese has melted in order to avoid the sauce mixture to separate. Add mushrooms and olives; transfer the prepared sauce to the top of a double broiler. Cover and keep warm over simmering water while you cook the pasta.

Cook pasta until "al dente"; drain the pasta well. Add butter to sauce and stir until it has melted; transfer the sauce to a large mixing bowl. Add the pasta and toss well; serve on individual plates and sprinkle with parsley and Parmesan cheese, if desired.

Pasta with Peas

Recipe from Jo Merklin

1 medium onion, sliced thin
Oil to sauté onion
1 can (15 oz.) small peas, with liquid
1 can (15 oz.) whole tomatoes (torn to pieces by hand)
Salt and pepper, to taste
Parmesan cheese, grated
1 lb. small shell pasta

Sauté onion in oil until golden brown; add peas, and tomatoes to mixture. Prepare pasta according to directions, and when al dente, drain and add pasta and pea mixture together. Top with grated Parmesan cheese.

The most indispensable ingredient of all good home cooking: love for those you are cooking for.
—Sophia Loren

Pasta with Tomatoes and Peas

Recipe from Rose Lambi

1 medium onion, sliced 1/8' thick
1 Tbl. olive oil
1 tsp. basil
2 tsp. salt
1 tsp. pepper
1 can (32 oz.) crushed tomato (Italian style)
1 can peas (do not drain liquid)
1/2 lb. spaghetti

In 3 qt. saucepan, sauté onions with olive oil until translucent. Add tomatoes, basil, salt, pepper; simmer for 30 minutes adding peas after 20 minutes of simmer time. While sauce is simmering, take 1/2 lb. spaghetti and break into 1/2-inch pieces; cook in boiling water with 2 tablespoons of salt. Drain; add to tomato sauce and serve with Parmesan cheese sprinkled on top.

Serves 4.

Inside-Out Ravioli

Recipe from Rose Lambi

2 cups bow-tie pasta
1 (10 oz) package frozen chopped spinach
1 Tbl. & 1/4 cup oil
1 lb. ground beef
1 medium onion, chopped
1 clove garlic, minced
16 oz. spaghetti sauce

8 oz. can tomato sauce
1/2 tsp. salt
1/8 tsp. pepper
1 cup Cheddar cheese, shredded
1 cup Italian breadcrumbs
2 eggs, well beaten

Cook spinach according to package directions; drain, reserving liquid and add water to make 1 cup total volume; set aside. Heat 1 tablespoon oil; sauté beef, onions and garlic until brown; add spinach liquid, spaghetti sauce, tomato sauce, salt and pepper. Simmer uncovered for 10 minutes. Combine spinach, bow-tie pasta, cheese, breadcrumbs, eggs and 1/4 cup oil; pour into greased 13 x 9 pan; top with sauce; bake at 350 degrees for 30 minutes; may be frozen and reheated. Serves 12-16.

For those who love it, cooking is at once child's play and adult joy. And cooking done with care is an act of love.
—Craig Claiborne

Ravioli (Homemade)

Recipe from Rose Lambi

<u>Filling:</u>
1 lb. ground pork
2 lb. ground beef
1 cup fresh parsley, chopped
1 cup spinach, chopped
1 cup seasoned breadcrumbs
2-1/2 cup grated Romano cheese
6 eggs
2 medium chopped onions
2 Tbl. salt
1 Tbl. pepper

<u>Dough:</u>
18 cups flour
12 eggs
3 Tbl. salt
6 cups warm water

Filling: Cook ground pork, ground beef and onions; drain all the fat and juices from the meat. In a large bowl add parsley, chopped spinach (make sure spinach is dry), breadcrumbs and grated cheese, 6 eggs, salt and pepper; mix thoroughly until all ingredients are combined. Place by teaspoon full on rolled out dough.

Dough: Mix all ingredients; knead dough until it becomes a fine smooth texture. Divide the dough into 2 equal parts and roll into 2 paper-thin sheets, the top one a little larger than the bottom. Working quickly so the dough doesn't dry out, place smaller sheet on floured board and place a heaping teaspoon of filling at 2-inch intervals; place larger sheet on top and cover loosely. Cut between the squares with a pastry cutter, making even squares. Press edges of dough firmly together with fingers and store on floured tray to dry until you are ready to cook. Cook ravioli in boiling water and when they float to the top, they are ready to drain and serve. A good meat sauce or marinara sauce is recommended on top of ravioli, and sprinkle with Parmesan or Romano cheese.

Serves 10-12.

Rice Balls

Recipe from Mary Midiri

1 lb. uncooked rice
1 cup breadcrumbs
2 eggs
1/2 cup grated cheese
1-1/2 lb. ground beef
Salt and pepper
1 onion, chopped
1/2 small can tomato paste with 1/4 can water
2 eggs, beaten
Additional breadcrumbs to roll balls in (about 3 cups)

Cook rice until tender; drain and cool slightly. Add 1 cup breadcrumbs, 2 eggs, 1/2 cup cheese, salt and pepper; mix well and set aside. Brown onion and meat in a little oil; add tomato paste and a little water; let simmer for 15 minutes, seasoning with salt and pepper; cool. Place 2 tablespoons cooked rice in the palm of your hand; make a well in rice and place 1 heaping tablespoon of meat mixture and mold rice around meat shaping into a ball. Dip balls in beaten eggs and roll in bread crumbs; fry in deep hot oil until golden brown on both sides. Do not fry too close together; remove from oil with a slotted spoon.

Yield 30 balls.

Spaghetti Meat Sauce

Recipe from Rose Lambi

2 lbs. ground round or hamburger
5 cloves garlic, chopped
1 medium onion, chopped
1 (15 oz.) can tomato paste
3 (15 oz.) cans tomato sauce
3 (15 oz.) cans chopped tomatoes
1/2 cup red cooking wine

1/2 cup dried or 8 leaves fresh basil
3 Tbl. sugar
1 Tbl. pepper
3 Tbl. salt
30 oz. water
(rinse empty cans by pouring water from can to can to remove remaining tomato sauces, then finally emptying in stockpot)

In large stockpot, brown ground round or hamburger with garlic, onions, salt and pepper. When ground round is cooked, add tomato paste and cook over medium high heat for 2 to 3 minutes, stirring frequently. Add tomato sauce and chopped tomatoes and stir for 2 minutes; add wine, basil, sugar, salt, pepper and water. When sauce begins to bubble, lower heat to low and cook for several hours with lid partially over pot stirring often.

Note: Salt and sugar may need to be altered because different batches of paste and tomato sauces have different acidity levels.

Tomato and Olive Penne

Recipe from Rose Lambi

1 lb. Penne or other short pasta
1/4 cup olive oil
2 garlic cloves, thinly sliced
2 cups cherry tomatoes, halved
1 tsp. dried oregano
1/2 tsp. crushed red pepper
1/2 tsp. salt and pepper
1/4 cup Kalamata olives, pitted & sliced
1/4 cup chopped fresh parsley
1/4 cup grated Parmesan cheese, plus more for serving

In a large pot of boiling salted water, cook the penne according to package instructions until al dente (about 13 minutes); drain. Meanwhile, heat olive oil over medium heat in large skillet; add garlic and cook until just golden. Add the cherry tomatoes, oregano, crushed red pepper, salt and pepper. Reduce heat to low and cook, stirring, until tomato juices run (about 3 minutes). Add penne, olives, parsley and 1/4 cup Parmesan to the skillet and toss to combine; serve immediately.   Serves 4.

Note: The cherry tomatoes cook just long enough to bring out their juice, which blends with the garlic-flavored olive oil to make one of the best-tasting pasta sauces.

Tortellini in Cream Sauce

Recipe from Rose Lambi

2 Tbl. butter
2 Tbl. flour
1 clove garlic, minced
2 cups Half-and-Half
12 oz. cooked tortellini
1 tsp. chicken bouillon granules
1/2 tsp. salt
1/4 tsp. white pepper
1 cup frozen peas
1-1/2 cups fresh sliced mushrooms

Melt butter in skillet over medium high heat, and garlic and flour, mix well. Warm Half-and-Half and add to flour mixture along with chicken bouillon; stir with wire whisk until sauce is smooth and thickens. Add salt, pepper, peas and mushrooms and cooked tortellini; if sauce is too thick, add white wine. Serve with grated Parmesan or Romano cheese with a salad and hard bread or roll for an easy gourmet meal in only minutes.

White Pasta Sauce

Recipe from Rose Lambi

1/2 cup (1 stick) butter
1 pint whipping cream
1 Tbl. flour, mixed with cold water
Salt and pepper
Optional: frozen peas, priscuitto ham, broccoli, asparagus spears or sliced mushrooms.

Melt butter in small saucepan; add whipping cream and let simmer for 5 to 10 minutes. Mix flour (approximately 1 tablespoon) with cold water (approximately 4 ounces), then add to butter & cream sauce slowly to thicken. Add salt & pepper to taste; add any of the optional items you wish and ladle over 1 pound of cooked pasta. Serve with Parmesan cheese.

Serves 4.

Zita Pasta Pomidoro

Recipe from Rose Lambi

1-1/2 cups butter, unsalted
1 clove garlic, minced
1/2 lb. fresh mushrooms, sliced
1 Tbl. salt
1/2 Tbl. pepper
1 bunch broccoli, cut into florettes
2 medium tomatoes, cut into 1-inch cubes

1/2 cup black olives
2 quart water
1 Tbl. vegetable or olive oil
1 lb. Zita pasta
1/2 cup Parmesan cheese, grated
Grated Parmesan cheese for topping

Melt butter in 2-quart saucepan or large skillet; add garlic, mushrooms, 1/2 tablespoon salt and pepper. Sauté over medium heat 5 to 8 minutes, or until mushrooms are softened. Stir in broccoli; reduce heat slightly. Cook uncovered 10 to 12 minutes, or until broccoli is tender but crisp. Do not overcook; add tomatoes and olives; simmer 10 minutes, or until tomatoes and broccoli are tender. Cover and keep warm over very low heat; this will make about 5-1/2 cups sauce.

Meanwhile, bring water, oil and remaining 1/2 tablespoon salt to a boil in large saucepan or stock pot; add pasta; cook 8 to 10 minutes or until done; drain.

In a large mixing bowl, toss drained pasta, sauce and 1/2 cup Parmesan cheese until well mixed; place mixture on a large serving platter and sprinkle with additional grated Parmesan cheese, if desired.

Note: I have made this pasta dish for years and it is a real crowd pleaser.

Serves 6.

Crawfish and Fettuccine

Recipe from Rose Lambi

8 oz. fettuccine
2 Tbl. butter
5 Tbl. red bell pepper, diced
5 Tbl. green bell pepper, diced
2 cups crawfish tails, cooked, peeled
2/3 cup onions, diced
1 cup (2 sticks) cold, unsalted butter pieces
4 Tbl. green onion, sliced
2/3 cup Creole tomato, diced
Red pepper, crushed, to taste
1 tsp. Creole seasoning

Cook fettuccine to al dente; rinse, lightly oil pasta and reserve water. Melt butter, sauté green & red peppers on high flame briefly; add cooked crawfish tails, onions, Creole seasoning and crushed red pepper. Sauté for 2 to 3 minutes; add Creole tomatoes & green onion; sauté briefly. Add piece by piece of cold, unsalted butter pieces to pan, swirling and stirring until all butter is melted. Check seasonings; remove from heat. Reheat reserved fettuccine in boiling salted water; drain well. Place in center of plate; spoon crawfish and sauce over pasta.

Serves 4.

Marinara Sauce

Recipe from Rose Lambi

2 cans (32 oz.) crushed tomatoes
5 cloves garlic, sliced
1/2 cup sweet fresh basil, chopped
1/4 cup olive oil
1 Tbl. salt
1 Tbl. pepper
2 Tbl. sugar
3 to 5 strips anchovies, chopped (optional)

In large pot or sauté pan over medium high heat, place olive oil and garlic, stirring until garlic is golden brown; add tomatoes and cook for additional 2 to 3 minutes. Add remaining ingredients; simmer for 30 to 45 minutes, stirring often.

Serves 4.

Pasta Con Broccoli

Recipe by Rose Lambi

8 oz. Cavatelli pasta (shell shaped)
1 bunch broccoli florettes
2 oz. tomato sauce
16 oz. Half & Half
1/4 cup butter
1/2 tsp. garlic, minced
2 oz. sliced mushrooms
Salt & pepper, to taste
1/4 cup grated or shredded Parmesan cheese

Cook pasta & broccoli florettes until pasta is half done; drain off water and place back into pot. Add cream, butter, garlic and tomato sauce; bring to a full boil. When noodles are fully cooked, add mushrooms and salt and pepper; stir into noodles. Remove from heat and add Parmesan cheese; toss and serve immediately.

Serves 4.

Pasta Capellini Olio

Recipe from Rose Lambi

6 oz. Capellini pasta
3 Tbl. olive oil
2 Tbl. sun-dried tomatoes, diced
2 tsp. garlic, crushed
2 Tbl. fresh basil leaves, diced
Salt, pepper and crushed red pepper, to taste
Parmesan cheese

Cook Capellini al dente, approximately 2-1/2 minutes; rinse and put to the side. In a large skillet, add oil, tomato, garlic, basil and spices; sauté slowly not to brown any of the ingredients. Heat thoroughly; add pasta and toss; serve on platter and sprinkle with Parmesan cheese.

Serves 2 entrees or 4 side dishes.

Pesto Sauce for Pasta

Recipe from Mary Midiri

4 cloves garlic
1/4 cup blanched almonds (toasted)
1 cup basil
Red pepper flakes, to taste
3/4 cup olive oil
Salt and pepper, to taste
1/2 cup Parmesan cheese

Blend in blender and pour over hot pasta!

Chocolate flatters you for awhile, it warms you for an instant;
then all of a sudden, it kindles a mortal fever in you.
—Marquise Marie de Sévigné

Spaghetti a´la Anchovy & Tomato

Recipe from Rose Lambi

1 lb. spaghetti, cooked al dente
3 oz. anchovies, chopped
1 lb. ripe tomatoes, cut in small pieces and removing seeds
3 oz. olive oil
1 clove garlic, whole or sliced in half
1 pepperoncini, cut in small pieces
3 oz. pitted brown olives
1-1/2 oz. capers, washed

Heat oil in large skillet and add garlic and pepperoncini; cover and continue to cook until garlic is golden brown. Discard the garlic and add anchovies; add tomatoes, olives and caper. Stir and let cook for about 8 minutes; taste for seasoning. Pour the spaghetti in skillet with the sauce, toss well and serve.

Note: Suggested olives are Gaeta or Nicoise, both found in Italian markets or specialty stores.

Zucchini Fettuccini

Recipe from Mary Midiri and Dawn Wilson

4 zucchini, chopped
1 pkg. frozen broccoli, chopped
1 lb. fettuccini noodles
1/2 cup (1 stick) butter
1 cup Parmesan cheese
1 pint Half-and-Half
Salt and pepper, to taste

Boil zucchini and broccoli in salted water for 15 minutes; add noodles to the same water and cook until tender. Drain; add butter; toss. Add cheese, Half-and-Half and salt and pepper to taste.

Serves 6 to 8.

Vegetables are a must on a diet. I suggest carrot cake, zucchini bread, and pumpkin pie.

—*Garfield*

Stuffed Spinach Shells

Recipe from Rose Lambi

1 pkg. jumbo macaroni shells
30 oz. creamed frozen spinach
1 to 1-1/2 lb. ground meat
24 oz. Ricotta cheese
12 oz. Mozzarella cheese, shredded
1 tsp. salt
1/4 tsp. pepper
Spaghetti sauce

Prepare shells by following direction cooking to very al dente; drain shells. Mix a few drops of oil on shells to prevent sticking to each other. Prepare spinach according to directions. Brown ground meat and drain; mix meat, spinach, cheeses and seasonings.

Ladle a thin layer of sauce on bottom of lasagna pan or 13 x 9 pan; stuff shells with mixture. In single layer, place shells in pan; ladle sauce on top of shells. Cover with foil and bake for 30 minutes (50 minutes, if frozen) at 350 degrees.

Serves 8 to 10.

SOUPS SALADS and Dressing

Helpful Hints

▲ For a spicy aroma, toss dried orange or lemon rinds into the fireplace.

▲ For a juicier hamburger, add cold water to the beef before grilling (1/2 cup to 1 pound of meat).

▲ When boiling corn, add sugar to the water instead of salt; salt will toughen the corn.

▲ Potatoes soaked in salt water for 20 minutes before baking will bake more rapidly.

▲ Use greased muffin tins as molds when baking stuffed green peppers.

▲ A few drops of lemon juice in the water will whiten boiled potatoes.

▲ Don't despair if you oversalt gravy. Stir in some instant mashed potatoes to repair the damage. Just add a little more liquid in order to offset the thickening.

▲ To keep cauliflower white while cooking, add a little milk to the water.

▲ Separate stuck-together glasses by filling the inside one with cold water and setting them in hot water.

Ambrosia Salad

Recipe from Rose Lambi

3/4 cup sour cream or vanilla yogurt
1 Tbl. sugar
1 can (20 oz.) chunk pineapple, in juice or syrup
1 can (11 oz.) mandarin oranges
1-1/2 cup seedless grapes
1 cup miniature marshmallows
1 cup flaked coconut
1/2 cup pecan pieces

Mix sour cream and sugar; add other ingredients; fold; chill.

Serves 14-16.

Antipasta Salad

Recipe from Norma Nichols

12 oz. noodles of your choice
3/4 cup Italian salad dressing
Small jar pimentos
1/4 lb. hard salami
1-1/4 cup black olives, sliced
1 small onion, sliced

Boil noodles per package directions; drain. Cut salami into strips; combine all ingredients; refrigerate.

Serves 4 to 6.

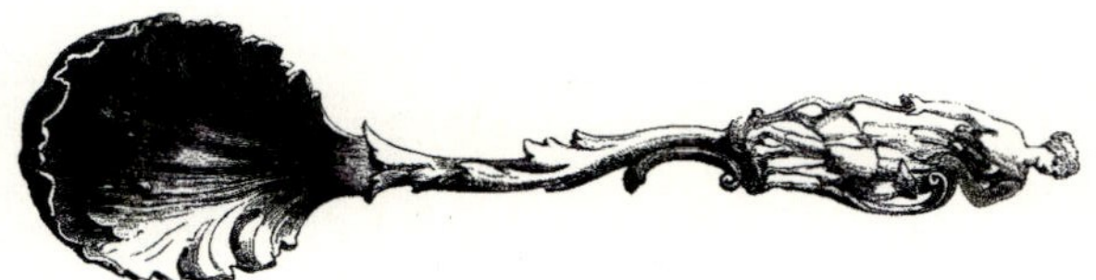

Chicken Lime Pasta Salad

Recipe from Mary Midiri

5 chicken breast, boneless
16 oz. Rotini or bow tie pasta
1 lime
1 bottle of Ceasar salad dressing
Pepper, to taste
1/4 cup grated Parmesan cheese

Grill or skillet-fry chicken. Take 1/2 zest and 1/2 of the lime juice and marinade chicken while cooking; cook pasta according to package directions; drain. Put in bowl with cut-up bite-sized pieces of your cooked chicken. Add the other half of lime juice and zest. Add dressing and cheese; toss and chill. A real crowd pleaser.

Quick and Easy Clam Chowder

Recipe from Mary Midiri

3 cans Cream of Potato soup
2 cans of New England Clam Chowder soup
1 can of minced clams (with juice)
1 qt. Half-and-Half
1/2cup (1 stick) butter

Sauté clams in butter; put all ingredients in crock pot and cook on low for 10 to 12 hours. Serve with salad and hot rolls.

Serves 6.

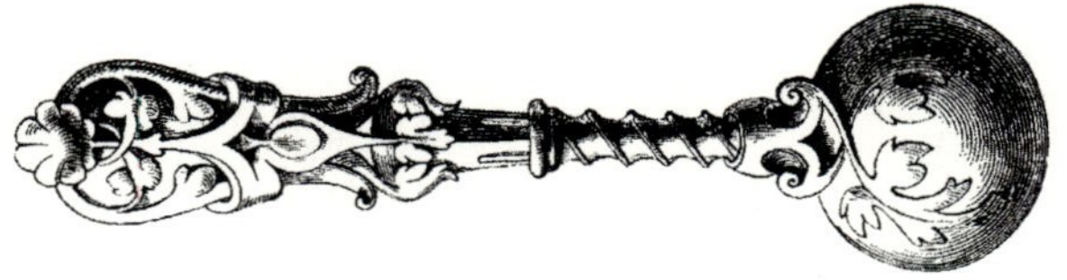

Cowboy Soup

Recipe from Mary Midiri

1 can stewed tomatoes (Italian Style)
1 can Veg-al
1 can tomato sauce with basil, garlic and oregano
1 can corn
1 can Spanish rice
1 can diced tomatoes with basil, garlic and oregano
1 lb. ground beef
1 onion, diced

Brown ground beef and onions; salt and pepper to taste. Add remaining ingredients and simmer for 30 minutes. Fast and easy, and everyone will love it.

If you want to make an apple pie from scratch, you must first create the universe.
—Carl Sagan

Cranberry Fluff

Recipe from Mary Midiri

1 bag cranberries, ground
1 cup sugar

Mix cranberries and sugar and refrigerate overnight.

Add:

3 cups minature marshmallows
3 cups chopped grapes (seedless)
1-1/4 cup of chopped nuts
8 oz. Cool Whip

Mix all together and serve; great with turkey or chicken.

Cranberry Jello Salad

Recipe from Mary Midiri

1 pkg. cherry Jello (6 oz.)
1 cup hot water
1 cup sugar
1 cup pineapple juice
1 tsp. lemon juice
1 can whole cranberry sauce
1 orange (ground) or 1 can mandarin oranges (drained)
1 cup drained crushed pineapple
1 cup pecans pieces

Dissolve Jello with hot water; add sugar, lemon and pineapple juice; chill till partially set; add the rest of the ingredients; chill and enjoy!

Note: Our family uses this recipe in lieu of cranberry sauce on Thanksgiving.

Cranberry-Jello Mold

Recipe from Rose Lambi

1 box cherry Jello (dissolved in 1/2 cup boiling water)
3 to 4 tsp. lemon juice
1 can whole cranberries
1/2 cup chopped pecans
1 small can crushed pineapple, drained
1/2 cup chopped celery

Let Jello mold part way (approximately 20 minutes); fold all the ingredients into Jello and mold completely.

Serves 8 to 12.

Good apple pies are a considerable part of our domestic happiness.
—Jane Austen

Famous Barr's French Onion Soup

Recipe from Rose Lambi

1 lb. 6 oz. peeled onions
3 oz. butter or margarine
1 tsp. ground pepper
1 Tbl. Spanish paprika
1-1/2 tsp. salt
2 bay leaves
1/2 cup all-purpose flour
1-1/2 quarts beef bouillon

Cut onions in half and slice with the grain about 1/8 inch thick; melt butter and add sliced onions. Sauté slowly for 20 minutes, stirring frequently; add paprika, pepper, salt, bay leaves and flour. Mix well, keeping flame low; stir while cooking for 5 minutes. Gradually add the hot beef bouillon while stirring, preferable with a wooden spoon. Simmer soup, covered, for at least 30 minutes. If a rich brown color is desired, add caramel coloring; season to taste with salt. Fill oven-proof casserole or individual oven-proof crooks with 8 ounces soup; top with thin slices of French bread and cover each serving with about 1-1/2 ounces grated Swiss cheese (Emmenthaler or Gruyere preferred). Place under broiler and melt cheese until golden brown.

This is by far, the best French Onion Soup!   Yield: 2 quarts.

Frozen Fruit Salad

Recipe from Mary Midiri

8 oz. cream cheese
3/4 cup sugar
10 oz. container Cool Whip
12 oz. frozen strawberries, thawed
20 oz. can crushed pineapple, drained
2 bananas, diced
1 cup chopped nuts (pecans and walnuts)

Cream cheese and sugar together; add strawberries and pineapple, then bananas and nuts. Fold in Cool Whip; place in 9 x 13 pan and freeze. Thaw 1/2 hour before serving.

Serves 12-16.

Fruit Salad

Recipe from Betty Guccione

1 box sugared strawberries
2 or 3 bananas sliced
1 can pineapple chunks drained
1 can peach pie filling

Mix all and chill.

Garden Pasta Salad

Recipe from Rose Lambi

Salad:
2 cups uncooked Rotini pasta
1/2 cup sliced black olives
1-1/2 cups small broccoli pieces
1/2 cup chopped bell pepper
1 cup diced tomato
1/2 cup chopped red onion
1/2 cup grated Parmesan cheese

Dressing:
2/3 cup olive oil
1 garlic clove, pressed
1/3 cup red wine vinegar
1 tsp. salt
1 tsp. dry mustard
Fresh ground pepper, to taste

Cook pasta according to package directions; rinse pasta, drain and cool. Transfer to mixing bowl; add remaining salad ingredients. In a separate bowl, whisk dressing ingredients until smooth and slightly thickened; pour over salad and toss lightly to combine. Cover and chill before serving. Serves 8.

Cooking is like love. It should be entered into with abandon or not at all.
—Harriet Van Horne

Garlic-Lemon Sauce

Recipe from Rose Lambi and Norma Nichols

**Full head of garlic,
peeled and crushed
Juice from 12 large lemons
Equal amount of Wesson Oil in ratio with lemon juice
Salt to set**

This sauce can be left in refrigerator for months. It is great on spedini, grilled breaded steaks or grilled chicken.

Grandma's Soup

Recipe from Betty Guccione

**3 tablespoons olive oil
1 head escarole
1 head endive
3 small garlic cloves chopped
2 cans cannellini beans
4 cans chicken broth
Frozen Meatballs (optional)**

In large pot sauté garlic cloves about 30 seconds until it gives off its aroma. Add escarole and endive and sauté until it is wilted. Add beans, chicken broth and salt to taste; if you like, you can add frozen meatballs. Cook until beans and meatballs are heated thoroughly.

Greek Pasta Salad

Recipe from Rose Lambi

1 lb. bow tie pasta, cooked according to directions
1 cup sliced black olives
1/2 cup diced red bell peppers
1 cup sliced scallions
1 cup diced yellow peppers
2 Tbl. fresh oregano
2 Tbl. chopped fresh basil
1 cup grated Romano cheese
1 Tbl. salt
1/2 Tbl. black pepper
1/2 Tbl. sugar
2 cups Feta cheese, crumbled,
mixed with your favorite vinaigrette

Combine all ingredients and mix well; serve cold. Garnish with pepperoncini, if desired.

Serves 6 to 8.

Marinated Mushroom Salad

Recipe from Rose Lambi

1 lb. mushrooms, thinly sliced
1 medium red onion, thinly sliced
1 medium celery stalk, finely chopped

<u>Marinade:</u>
1 cup olive oil
1/2 cup tarragon wine vinegar
1 tsp. dry mustard
1/2 tsp. dried thyme
1/8 tsp. salt
1/8 tsp. ground pepper
1/2 tsp. dried oregano
1/2 tsp. dried basil

Blend marinade ingredients in a blender. Combine mushrooms, red onions and celery in 3-quart dish; pour marinade over ingredients and toss. Cover and refrigerate overnight, stirring twice; drain before serving.

Hamburger Minestrone Soup

Recipe from Mary Midiri

1 lb. ground chuck
1 cup chopped onion
1 large clove garlic, chopped
1-1/2 qt. water
1 cup cubed potatoes
1 cup sliced carrots
1 cup diced celery
1 cup shredded cabbage

1 (20 oz.) can whole or crushed tomatoes with juice
1 small bay leaf
1/2 tsp. dried thyme
1/4 tsp. dried basil
3 tsp. salt
1/8 tsp. pepper
1/4 cup uncooked rice or 3 oz. uncooked spaghetti,
broken into bite-sized pieces
Grated Parmesan cheese

In a large stockpot cook beef, onions and garlic until lightly brown; add water, potatoes, carrots, celery, cabbage and tomatoes with juice. Bring to a boil; add all the spices; stir and simmer for 15 minutes. Add rice or pasta; reduce heat and cover and simmer for 30 minutes or until vegetables and rice is cooked. Remove bay leaf; sprinkle with Parmesan cheese and serve.

Serves 6 to 8.

Great main dish served with green salad and hot rolls!

Italian Wedding Soup by Rachel Ray

Recipe from Dawn Wilson

3 Tbl. olive oil
4 carrots, sliced
4 stalks of celery, sliced
1 small onion, diced
3 big cans of chicken stock
2 cups of water
Acini de peppi pasta
Spinach, chopped

1/2 lb. hamburger
1/2 lb. ground pork
1/2 lb. ground veal
1/2 cup breadcrumbs
1/2 cup parmesan cheese
1/2 tsp. nutmeg
1 clove garlic, chopped
1 egg

In a large soup pot, add olive oil and sauté onion, carrots, celery until clear. Meanwhile, in a medium mixing bowl, mix meatloaf mixture, nutmeg, egg, breadcrumbs, nutmeg, garlic, salt and pepper and form into tiny meatballs. Add water and chicken stock to soup pot with vegetable and bring to a boil. Once boiling, add meatballs and pasta and simmer for 40 minutes. Add spinach and pasta and continue to simmer for 30 minutes.

Serves 8-10.

Food is our common ground, a universal experience.
—James Beard

Mayfair Dressing

Recipe from Rose Lambi

2 cans flat anchovies, rinsed in hot water
2 Tbl. mustard
1/2 medium onion, quartered
1 rib celery, stripped
1 tsp. sugar
1/2 tsp. lemon juice
1/2 tsp. pepper
1 tsp. Accent seasoning
3 eggs
2 cups vegetable or canola oil

Blend in blender adding raw eggs (1 at a time) and oil (1/4 cup at a time). Can be kept in refrigerator for 1 week after making. You will get many compliments with this dressing.

Mayfair Dressing

Recipe from Jo Merklin

2 cloves garlic, chopped
1/4 small onion, sliced
3 Tbl. water
4 small ribs celery, sliced
2 Tbl. prepared mustard
2 eggs
2-1/4 cup vegetable oil
2 oz. canned anchovies
1 tsp. black pepper

Put onion, celery, eggs, anchovies, pepper, garlic and mustard in blender; blend on high speed 1 to 2 minutes. Slowly, drop by drop, add oil.

Yield 32 (tablespoon) servings.

Pasta Fugioli Soup

Recipe from Mary Midiri

1 Tbl. olive oil
2 cloves garlic
1 onion, chopped
1 small zucchini, sliced
1 can diced tomatoes (basil, garlic and oregano)
2 cans beef broth
2 cup water
1 tsp. dry basil

1/2 tsp. dry oregano
1/4 tsp. black pepper
2 to 3 dashes Tabasco sauce
1 can red kidney beans (rinse and drained)
1 cup fresh spinach leaves (minced)
2 Tbl. fresh parsley
3/4 cup shell or elbow macaroni
1/2 cup Parmesan cheese

Heat oil and add garlic, onion and carrots sautéing until onion is tender. Stir in zucchini, tomato, broth, water and spices; cover and heat until boiling. Reduce and cook for 15 minutes; stir in kidney beans, spinach and parsley. Cover and cook 15 minutes more; increase heat and add macaroni and cook 10 minutes. Serve in bowls and sprinkle cheese on top; serve with hard crusty rolls.

The dangerous person in the kitchen is the one who goes
rigidly by weights, measurements, thermometers, and scales.
—X. Marcel Boulestin

Minestrone Soup á la Dawn

Recipe from Dawn Wilson

1 yellow large onion
3 Tbl. olive oil
2 to 3 lbs. hamburger
1 small head cabbage, sliced thin
2 Tbl. garlic, chopped
2 (15 oz.) cans diced tomatoes, with the juice
10 beef bouillon cubes
1 (15 oz.) can red kidney beans, drained
4 potatoes, peeled and diced
6 carrots, peeled and sliced

5 stalks of celery, sliced
1 medium zucchini, diced (optional)
1 tsp. thyme
2 tsp. Italian seasoning
1 tsp. parsley flakes
1 tsp. salt
1 tsp. pepper
2 to 3 quarts water or enough to fill stockpot to 3/4 level
1/2 lb. small pasta such as stars, orzo or tiny flowers

Dice one large yellow onion; put in soup pot and simmer with olive oil. Once the onion starts to turn clear, add 1 tablespoon of the garlic. Add hamburger and cook with the olive oil mixture until browned; drain grease. Add all remaining ingredients except the pasta and cabbage, bring to a boil; let boil 15 minutes then reduce to simmer for 1 to 2 hours. Add pasta and cabbage during last 30 minutes of simmer.

Food, it appeared, could be important. It could be an event. It had secrets.
—Anthony Bourdain

Pasta Fugioli

Recipe from Rose Lambi

2 lb. ground beef
1/2 medium onion, diced
8 oz. baby carrots, sliced 1/8-inch thick pieces
3 stalks celery, sliced 1/8-inch thick
2 cans (15 oz.) northern beans
2 cans (15 oz.) kidney beans
2 cans (15 oz.) diced tomatoes with green chillis
2 Tbl. salt
1 Tbl. pepper
1 Tbl. sweet basil
1 to 2 cups D'Italia pasta

In stockpot, brown beef and onion; drain off fat; add carrots and celery, and sauté for 3 minutes. Add remaining ingredients except pasta; stir, bring to a boil then simmer for 45 minutes to 1 hour. Boil pasta in water with 3 tsp. salt; drain and add to stock pot. Serve with Parmesan cheese sprinkled on top.

This is an Italian version of chili but oh, so good. You will never eat chili again!

Mock Pasta House Salad

Recipes by Rose Lambi

1 head iceberg lettuce
1/2 head romaine lettuce
1 medium thinly sliced red onion
6 oz. artichoke hearts
1 oz. pimento
1/2 cup Parmesan cheese
salt and pepper

Dressing:
4 oz. olive oil
1 oz. red wine vinegar

Mix and serve.

Serves 8 for entrée or 16 side dishes.

Mom's Potato Salad

Recipe from Rose Lambi

5 lb. red potatoes
3 stalks celery, stripped and chopped
1/2 medium onion, chopped
2 to 3 eggs, hard boiled
3 Tbl. salt
1 Tbl. ground pepper
2 tsp. celery seeds
1 cup mayonnaise
2 Tbl. mustard
3 to 5 Tbl. water

Boil potatoes & eggs in boiling water for 12 to 20 minutes; rinse with cold water and let potatoes and eggs sit in cold water for 20 to 30 minutes to cool. Meanwhile, chop celery and onions. Remove the skins from the potatoes and cut into potato salad size; place in mixing bowl. Add chopped hard boiled eggs, celery onion, salt, pepper and celery seeds. Mix mayonnaise, mustard and water together until smooth and runny like ranch dressing; add more water if needed to reach that consistency. Pour into potato mixture and blend well. Place in a serving bowl, sprinkle with paprika, cover with wrap and refrigerate for several hours.

Serves 8 to 12.

Potato, Tomato and Green Bean Salad

Recipe from Rose Lambi

2 large ripe tomatoes
2 lbs. red potatoes
1-1/2 lb. fresh green beans
1-1/2 Tbl. dried sweet basil
1-1/2 cup olive oil
3/4 cup red wine vinegar
1 tsp. salt
1 tsp. pepper
1 Tbl. sugar

Wash potatoes and green beans; cut unpeeled potatoes in quarter and boil until cooked, but firm. Drain and set aside to cool. Pinch ends of beans and steam them for 10 minutes. Cut tomatoes into 1/2-inch wedges; place potatoes, green beans and tomatoes into large bowl. In a separate bowl, whisk all other ingredients together and pour over tomatoes and vegetables. Chill in refrigerator for several hours;

This is a great substitute for salad and vegetable.

Stewed Chicken Soup

Recipe from Dawn Wilson

5 to 6 lb. chicken
4 stalks celery, sliced
4 stalks carrots, sliced
1 onion, chopped
5 potatoes, peeled and diced
1 Tbl. garlic
1-1/2 cup corn
1 Tbl. flaked parsley
1 cup Acini de Pepi Pasta
5 chicken bouillon cubes
Salt and pepper to taste

Boil chicken pieces for 30 minutes. Add all ingredients above and continue to boil for 15 minutes. Reduce heat; remove chicken and let cool separately. Once cooled, remove from bone and place small pieces of chicken back into pot with remaining ingredients; simmer for 45 minutes. Add Acini de Pepi pasta if desired and simmer 15 more minutes until pasta is cooked.

Betty's Strawberry Jello

Recipe from Mary Midiri

2 large pkg. strawberry Jello
1-1/2 cup water
1 can (16 oz.) crushed pineapple with juice
2 pkg. frozen strawberries

Mix and chill till above until partially thickened; add 4 bananas (mashed).

Pour half of the mixture into 9 x 13 pan and chill until gelled. Add 12 oz. sour cream over Jello; add remainder of Jello and refrigerate. This is GOOD!

Strange to see how a good dinner and feasting reconciles everybody.

—Samuel Pepys

Tomato and Red Onion Salad

Recipe from Rose Lambi

2 lbs. red ripe tomatoes
1 large red onion
2/3 cup olive oil
1/3 cup red wine vinegar
1 tsp. sugar
2 Tbl. oregano
1 Tbl. salt
1 tsp. pepper
1 small can anchovies (optional)
1/3 cup cold water

Slice tomatoes into 1-inch wedges and cut onion into thin long strips. Place in a large bowl and add all the other ingredients; mix well until tomatoes and onions are thoroughly soaked. Add anchovies if desired; refrigerate for several hours to chill. Serve with garlic cheese bread or plain Italian sliced bread.

Note: To expedite the chill process substitute 5 to 6 ice cubes instead of cold water.

Tomato, Cucumber and Bread Cube Salad

Recipe from Betty Guccione

3 cups Italian bread (can also use bagels)
3 medium tomatoes, chopped
1/2 medium red onion, sliced thin
1/2 cucumber, cut into small chunks
1/4 cup basil
2 Tbl. parsley
2 garlic cloves, minced
2 Tbl. red or white wine vinegar
2 Tbl. olive oil
Salt and pepper to taste

Combine bread cubes, tomatoes, onion, cucumber, basil, parsley and garlic in mixing bowl. Stir vinegar, olive oil, salt and pepper in small bowl; spoon dressing over salad tossing gently to coat. Let stand at room temperature for 15 minutes to allow flavors to blend.

Deli Salad

Recipe from Rose Lambi

1/2 lb. Rainbow Rotini pasta,
cooked according to directions
5 oz. pepperoni stick, sliced thin
9 oz. artichoke hearts
1 cup fresh sliced cauliflower
1 cup fresh sliced broccoli
1 cup small cubed Monterey cheese
1/2 cup sliced green onions
3/4 cup olive oil
1/4 cup red wine vinegar
1/2 tsp. Italian seasoning

Combine all ingredients and mix well; chill for several hours or a day before serving.

Serves 6-8.

Garlic-Lemon Sauce

Recipe from Gwen Guccione

2 Tbl. crushed garlic
1 cup fresh lemon juice
3/4 cup vegetable oil
2 Tbl. chopped parsley or flakes
1/2 tsp. pepper
1 tsp. salt

Great brushed on breaded steaks and grilled chicken.

All Italians can sing. All Italians can cook.
—Angelo Pellegrini

Potato Salad á la Dawn

Recipe from Dawn Wilson

5 lb. new potatoes (leave the skin on)
1 large container of small curd cottage cheese
1 large jar real mayonnaise
3 bunches of green onions, sliced
Parsley, chopped fine

Boil potatoes with skin on until tender; drain and let cool. Slice potatoes into thin slices; layer potato slices and all above ingredients twice in a 9 x 13 pan. Stir when ready to serve.

Refrigerate.

Minestrone Soup

Recipe from Norma Nichols

1 clove garlic
2 cups beef broth
1-1/4 cup water
1 cup celery, sliced thin
1 small zucchini, sliced thin about a cup
3 small red potatoes, diced
1-15 oz. can red kidney beans, drained
1-28 oz. can diced tomatoes with juice
1-15 oz. can corn, drained
1/2 to 3/4 cup uncooked noodles of choice

Heat broth and water; add all vegetables and noodles; heat to boiling. Reduce heat; cover and simmer 20 to 30 minutes, stirring often, until potatoes and noodles are tender. Serve with cheese.

Serves 4 to 6.

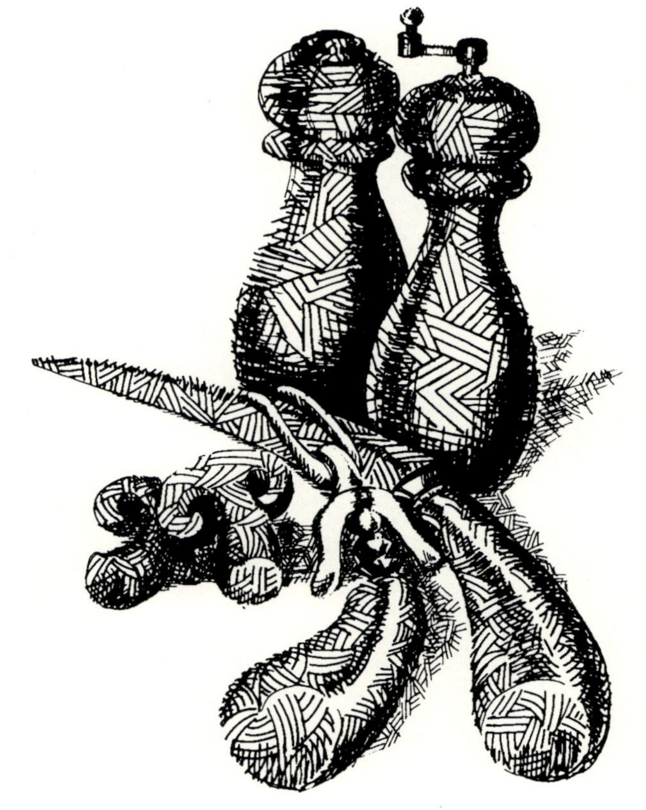

VEGETABLES

Helpful Hints

▲ To avoid toughened beans or corn, add salt midway through cooking.

▲ Tomatoes added to roasts will help to naturally tenderize them. Tomatoes contain an acid that works well to break down meats.

▲ Whenever possible, cut meats across the grain; they will be easier to eat and have a better appearance.

▲ When frying meat, sprinkle paprika over it to turn it golden brown.

▲ Over-ripe bananas can be peeled and frozen in a plastic container until it's time to bake bread or cake.

▲ When baking bread, a small dish of water in the oven will help keep the crust from getting too hard or brown.

▲ When baking in a glass pan, reduce the oven temperature by 25 degrees.

▲ When baking bread, you get a finer texture if you use milk. Water makes a coarser bread.

▲ If your biscuits are dry, it could be from too much handling, or the oven temperature may not have been hot enough.

Broccoli Casserole

Recipe from Rose Lambi

40 oz. broccoli, chopped, cooked & drained
2 cans Cream of Chicken soup (undiluted)
1 cup mayonnaise
2 to 3 Tbl. lemon juice
2 cups shredded cheddar cheese
1 cup breadcrumbs
4 Tbl. butter, melted
2 tsp. seasoned salt

Grease 13 x 9 pan with butter & pepper; place broccoli in pan; mix soup, mayo, lemon juice and spread over broccoli. Sprinkle with cheese, then crumbs; drizzle with butter, then seasoned salt.

Bake at 350 degrees for 30 to 40 minutes.

Serves 12+.

Broccoli Casserole á la Betty

Recipe from Betty Guccione

1 pkg. frozen chopped broccoli
1/4 lb. grated cheddar cheese
1 can condensed potato soup

Thaw vegetables, slightly combine with soup and half of cheese. Place in buttered casserole; sprinkle remaining cheese on top. Bake in 350 oven for 1/2 hour until brown and bubbly.

Broccoli Casserole

Recipe from Mary Midiri

**2 10 oz. boxes of frozen broccoli,
thawed and well drained
1 can Cream of Mushroom soup
1 cup mayonnaise
2 eggs, beaten
2 cups Cheddar cheese, shredded**

Mix all together and pour into a greased casserole dish; crush 1 sleeve of Ritz crackers in a sealed plastic bag. Pour 1/2 cup melted butter over crackers and mix well in bag. Place over broccoli in dish; bake at 350 degrees for 35 to 45 minutes.

Dinner is to a day what dessert is to dinner.
—Michael Dorris

Broccoli Italian Style

Recipe from Rose Lambi

**2 bunches of broccoli
3/4 cup olive oil
3 cloves garlic, quartered
1/2 cup Italian-style breadcrumbs
1/2 cup grated Romano cheese
Salt & pepper, to taste**

Cut broccoli florettes from stem and boil for 10 to 15 minutes; drain, place in a bowl. In a large sauté pan add oil and garlic; cook on medium heat. Mix breadcrumbs and cheese together, then sprinkle on top of broccoli. When the oil is very hot and the garlic has turned a dark golden color, remove the garlic with a spoon, pour oil over the top of the broccoli and breadcrumb mixture. Serve immediately.

Serves 4.

Carrots Eleganté

Recipe from Rose Lambi

**1 lb. carrots, sliced into 1/8-inch slices or use baby
carrots, whole
1/4 cup butter
1/2 cup golden raisins
3 Tbl. honey
1/4 tsp. ginger
1 Tbl. lemon juice
1/2 cup sliced almonds**

Cook carrots, covering within 1/2-inch boiling water, for
8 minutes; drain. Add ingredients except almonds.
Bake uncovered for 35 minutes at 375 degrees;
sprinkle with almonds.

Serves 4.

Carrots Grand Marnier

Recipe from Rose Lambi

**2 lb. carrots, cleaned and cut into 1/2-inch thick slices
1/2 tsp. salt
6 Tbl. butter, divided
1 cup sugar
12 oz. orange marmalade
3/4 cup Grand Marnier
Nutmeg
4 medium oranges, halved with pulp and pith removed**

Combine carrots and salted water to cover carrots in
a pan; cover and cook over medium heat 35 minutes;
drain and set aside. Melt butter in a large skillet over
medium heat; add sugar and marmalade and simmer about
10 minutes or until sugar is melted. Stir in carrots and 1/2
cup Grand Marnier; simmer uncovered about 30 minutes.
Add remaining Grand Marnier; sprinkle with nutmeg and
serve in hollowed scalloped orange shells.

Serves 8.

Eggplant Parmesan

Recipe from Rose Lambi

1 large eggplant
Salt, to taste
1-1/2 quart Italian tomato sauce
2 cups grated Provelone cheese or Provel ropes

Breadcrumb mixture:
3 cups Italian seasoned breadcrumbs
1 cup Romano or Parmesan cheese
1 Tbl. garlic powder
3 Tbl. sweet basil
2 tsp. salt
2 tsp. pepper

Trim outer skin off eggplant; cut eggplant in half lengthwise into 1/8-inch thick slices and salt each piece. Place in colander with a pie pan underneath for drainage for 2-3 hours in refrigerator. Rinse off eggplant and pat dry with paper towel. In shallow bowl, mix breadcrumb mixture. In pie plate, beat eggs; dip eggplant in egg mixture; then in breadcrumb mixture until eggplant is breaded entirely. In a sauté pan, add a few tablespoons of vegetable oil and heat to medium high heat. Cook eggplant on both sides until golden brown, remove and drain on paper towel. In baking dish, put a small amount of sauce on bottom, then begin layering with eggplant pieces side by side, small amount of Provelone cheese, then sauce. Continue layering eggplant; top with remaining Provelone cheese and bake at 350 degrees for 20 minutes.

Serves 4.

Green Bean Casserole á la Betty

Recipe from Betty Guccione

2 large bags frozen French style green beans, thawed
1 large can French onion rings
1 can Campbell's Cheddar Cheese soup
1/4 cup milk

In large casserole, layer one bag of green beans. Heat soup in pan with 1/4 cup milk; pour half of mix over green beans. Put half of the onion rings over the soup mix and cover with the second bag of green beans; pour the rest of the soup over the second layer and top with the remaining onion rings. Bake at 350 degrees until hot and bubbly (about 30 minutes).

Serves 8.

A good meal makes a man feel more charitable toward the world than any sermon.
—Arthur Pendenys

Green Beans Italiano

Recipe from Rose Lambi

1 lb. fresh Italian Green Beans
1 cup ripe tomatoes, chopped
1/4 cup olive oil
1 garlic clove, chopped
1 tsp. basil
1 tsp. salt
1 tsp. pepper

Clean and snap both ends off of beans; steam green beans for 10 to 15 minutes. In a large skillet add oil, tomatoes, chopped garlic, basil, salt and pepper; blend together. Add green beans; cook until thoroughly heated.

Note: May substitute green beans for Italian green beans.

Serves 4.

Marinated Vegetables

Recipe from Mary Midiri

Cauliflower	**DRESSING:**
Broccoli	**1 cup vegetable oil**
Artichoke hearts	**1 cup vinegar**
Green olives	**1 Tbl. accent**
Black olives	**1/2 cup Wish Bone Italian dressing**
Baby corn (1 can;drained)	**1 Tbl. dill**
Mushrooms	**1 tsp. sugar**
Grape tomatoes	**1 tsp. garlic salt**
	1 tsp. black pepper

Mix dressing and pour over your veggies; refrigerate for several hours or overnight. I put everything in a storage bag and toss it everytime I go in the refrigerator. This is really, really good!!!!!

When we no longer have good cooking in the world, we will have no literature,
not high and sharp intelligence, nor friendly gatherings, no social harmony.
—Marie-Antoine Careme

Mary's Party Potatoes

Recipe from Mary Midiri

8 to 10 potatoes, cooked
8 oz. cream cheese
12 oz. sour cream
1/2 tsp. garlic salt

Mash one potato at a time, adding a little milk with each one. Add cream cheese, sour cream and garlic salt. Spray a 9 x 13 pan with vegetable or canola oil; put potatoes in pan and dot with pads of butter. Sprinkle with paprika; bake for 30 minutes at 350 degrees.

A good cook is like a sorceress who dispenses happiness.
—Elsa Schiaperelli

Picnic Carrots

Recipe from Betty Guccione

1 lb. carrots, sliced 1/4-inch thick
1 onion, thinly sliced
1 green pepper, thinly sliced
1 can tomato soup
1 tsp. salt
1/2 tsp. pepper
1/2 cup oil
1/2 cup sugar
1/2 cup vinegar

Boil carrots (do not overcook; carrots should be firm). In separate saucepan heat to boil soup, salt, pepper, oil, sugar and vinegar; pour over cooked carrots, onions and green pepper. Refrigerate. Carrots should be served cold.

Escalloped Potatoes

Recipe from Rose Lambi

2 lb shredded hash brown potatoes
1/2 medium onion, chopped fine
2 cup (16 oz.) sour cream
1 can Cream of Chicken soup, undiluted
3 cups Cheddar cheese, shredded
Salt and pepper, to taste
1/2 cup butter, melted
2 cups corn flakes, crushed

Spray 13 x 9 glass pan with non-stick spray; mix thawed hash brown potatoes, sour cream, soup, onion, 2 cups cheese and salt and pepper in large mixing bowl. Spread evenly in pan; sprinkle top with remaining 1 cup cheese. Mix melted butter and crushed corn flakes in a small bowl, then spoon evenly over cheese. Bake at 350 degrees uncovered for 45 to 50 minutes.

Serves 12 to 15.

Golden Parmesan Potatoes

Recipe from Rose Lambi

6 large white potatoes
1/4 cup all-purpose flour
1/4 cup Parmesan cheese
1 tsp. salt
1/8 tsp. pepper
1/2 cup butter

Scrub potatoes and cut into quarters lengthwise leaving skins on; let soak in water. Mix all dry ingredients in a plastic bag; melt butter in 13 x 9 pan. Dip wet potatoes a couple at a time in dry mixture and shake bag. Place coated potatoes in buttered pan in a single layer.

Bake at 375 degrees for 1 hours, turning once or twice during baking; remove from oven when golden brown; sprinkle with parsley and serve.

Serves 8 to 10.

Sautéed Cabbage

Recipe from Betty Guccione

1/2 head of small green cabbage
1/2 head of small red cabbage
2 cloves fresh garlic
1 small shallot
2 medium tomatoes
1 Tbl. butter
2 Tbl. olive oil
Salt and pepper, to taste

In large skillet melt butter and oil; add chopped garlic. Chop cabbage and shallot in small pieces and add to pan. Sauté about 5 minutes and add chopped tomatoes, salt and pepper. Cook another 5 to 10 minutes until cabbage is done. Do not overcook. Serve immediately.

Serves 4.

Spinach Italiano

Recipe from Rose Lambi

1 cup water
1 lb. fresh spinach
1 cup chopped tomatoes
1/4 cup olive oil
2 cloves garlic, chopped
1 tsp. oregano
1 tsp. salt
1 tsp. pepper

Wash spinach and cut off stems. In a saucepan, add tomatoes, oil, chopped garlic, oregano, salt and pepper; cook on medium heat for 2 minutes. Add spinach. When spinach is wilted, place all in bowl and serve immediately.

Serves 4.

Stuffed Artichokes

Recipe by Rose Lambi

4 large artichokes
2 to 3 Tbl. olive oil
1/2 medium onion, minced fine
2 cloves garlic, minced
3 Tbl. parsley, minced
2 cup seasoned breadcrumbs
1 cup Parmesan cheese
Salt and pepper
4 Tbl. butter

Cut stem off artichoke so it will be flat on bottom; cut about 1 inch off top of artichoke; rinse and turn upside down to drain. Sauté onion, garlic, and parsley in olive oil until golden; add to breadcrumbs and cheese and mix well adding salt and pepper to taste. Spread each leaf and stuff well with mixture, placing any remaining mixture in a small mound on top of each artichoke. Drizzle approximately 1 tablespoon melted butter over the top of each; place in deep pan and add about 1 inch of water. Cover with lid and steam for about 45 minutes, checking during cooking to add more water, if necessary.

Can serve with drawn butter for dipping, if desired. Eat the meaty part of each leaf, which is closest to the center of artichoke. When you reach the fuzzy part of artichoke near the heart of the artichoke, remove the fuzzy part with a spoon or fork, then cut heart in pieces and enjoy.

Stuffed Zucchini

Recipe from Rose Lambi

3 medium size zucchini
2 Tbl. butter
1 cup mushrooms, chopped
2 Tbl. flour
1/2 tsp. salt
1/4 tsp. oregano
1 cup Provolone cheese, shredded
2 Tbl. chopped pimento

Cook zucchini in salted, boiling water about 10 minutes or until tender; drain. Cut lengthwise; scoop to within 1/4 inch of skin. Chop scooped center portion.

Melt butter in large skillet; sauté mushrooms 3 minutes or until tender. Stir in flour and seasoning; remove from heat and stir in cheese and pimento. Stir in chopped zucchini.

Fill shells, using about 1/4 cup filling for each. Broil several inches from source of heat until hot and bubbly, 3 to 5 minutes; serve immediately.

Serves 6.

Sweet and Sour Zucchini

Recipe from Mary Midiri

3 to 5 cups sliced zucchini
2 Tbl. oil (for frying)
3 cloves garlic, sliced or minced
1/4 cup sugar
1/4 cup white vinegar
1/4 cup water

Wash and cut 3 to 5 cups zucchini into 1/4-inch round disks; fry in a little oil until golden brown. Drain on paper towel; salt and pepper. Sauté 3 cloves garlic in same skillet; add 1/4 cup vinegar, 1/4 cup of sugar and 1/4 cup of water. Stir until sugar dissolves. Place fried zucchini in shallow dish and pour sweet sour mixture over zucchini; serve cold.

Note: Best if refrigerated overnight.

Sweet Potato Casserole

Recipe from Rose Lambi

3 cups sweet potatoes, mashed
1 cup sugar
2 eggs
1/2 cup milk
1/2 tsp. salt
1-1/2 tsp. vanilla
1 cup brown sugar
1/2 cup flour
1 cup pecans, chopped
1/2 cup butter, softened not melted

Cook and mash sweet potatoes; combine with sugar, eggs, milk, salt and vanilla; spray a 2-quart casserole with non-stick spray and pour mixture in casserole.

Mix together brown sugar, flour and butter; mix pecans in by hand. Spread mixture over sweet potatoes; bake at 350 degrees for 35 minutes.

Zucchini Parmegiana

Recipe from Norma Nichols

1 large zucchini, 1/2-inch slices
1 egg, unbeaten
2 Tbl. water
Italian breadcrumbs
Vegetable oil
8 oz. tomato sauce
1/2 cup grated Parmesan cheese
8 oz. shredded Mozzarella cheese

Beat egg with water; dip zucchini in egg mixture. Coat with breadcrumbs. In oil, sauté zucchini until brown on the outside and fork tender. In a 2-quart casserole layer half of the zucchini, half tomato sauce, half Parmesan and half Mozzarella; repeat sequence layering and bake 350 degrees for 25 to 30 minutes.

Serves 4 to 6.

Marinated Veggies

Recipe from Mary Midiri

1/2 cup chopped onion
1 can red beans, drained
1 can surprisingly sweet corn, drained
1/2 red and 1/2 green pepper, chopped
1 jar pimento, chopped
1 cup celery, chopped
9 pkg. Sweet and Low
1 cup vinegar
1/3 cup oil
1/2 tsp. pepper

Mix and toss sweet and low, vinegar, oil and pepper with veggies; refrigerate for several days.

Note: You can substitute whichever vegetables you wish; these are what I use.

Stuffed Artichokes

Recipe from Gwen Guccione

Cut one inch off the top of each artichoke; remove outer lower leaves and cut off stem from 4 medium size artichokes. Cover with cold water with 1 teaspoon salt; let stand 30 minutes.

Meanwhile, mix:

1 cup breadcrumbs
1 clove garlic, sliced thin
2 tsp. grated parmesan cheese
1 tsp. chopped parsley
1 tsp. salt
1/2 tsp. pepper

Wash artichokes, spread leaves and place 3 slices of garlic in each artichoke. Place crumb mixture between and on to of artichokes. Place artichokes in heavy roaster with 2 cups water; sprinkle 3 tablespoons olive oil over the tops of artichokes. Cover and cook about 30 minutes or until leaves are tender.

Nothing would be more tiresome than eating and drinking if God had not made them a pleasure.

—Voltaire

INDEX

Chocolate

Coconut

Marshmallows

Mushrooms

Whipped Topping or Whipping Cream

Please send _______copies of *Sorella's Kitchen*

@$14.95 (U.S.) each $_______________

Plus postage/handling @ $3.50 each $_______________

Missouri residents add sales tax @ $1.25 each $_______________

Check or money order Total $_______________

Name:

____

Address:

____

City: ________________________State: _________ Zip: _______________

Phone: (day)_________________________(night)_______________________

Mail to:
Rose Lambi • 1515 Hibernation Hollow • Wentzville, MO 63385
For more information, please E-mail Rose Lambi
rlambi@centurytel.net

Please send _______copies of *Sorella's Kitchen*

@$14.95 (U.S.) each $_______________

Plus postage/handling @ $3.50 each $_______________

Missouri residents add sales tax @ $1.25 each $_______________

Check or money order Total $_______________

Name:

____

Address:

____

City: ________________________State: _________ Zip: _______________

Phone: (day)_________________________(night)_______________________

Mail to:
Rose Lambi • 1515 Hibernation Hollow • Wentzville, MO 63385
For more information, please E-mail Rose Lambi
rlambi@centurytel.net